CW00670494

The Zombies

Claes Johansen

Also by Claes Johansen
PROCOL HARUM - BEYOND THE PALE

The Zombies

Hung Up
On A
Dream

a biography - 1962-1967

Claes Johansen

saf publishing

saf publishing

First published in 2001 by SAF Publishing Ltd

SAF Publishing Ltd
Unit 7, Shaftesbury Centre, 85 Barlby Road,
London. W10 6BN
ENGLAND

www.safpublishing.com

ISBN 0 946719 34 9

Text copyright © 2001 Claes Johansen

The right of Claes Johansen to be identified as the author of this
work has been asserted by him in accordance with the Copyright,
Designs and Patents Act, 1988.

All rights reserved. No part of this publication may be transmitted
in any form, or by any means, electronic, photocopying, recording or otherwise, without the prior permission of the publisher.

All lyrics quoted are for review, study or critical purposes.

A CIP catalogue record for this book is available from the British
Library.

Printed in England by:
The Cromwell Press, Trowbridge, Wiltshire.

Acknowledgements

The author would like to thank Rod Argent, Paul Atkinson, Colin Blunstone, Hugh Grundy, Chris White, John DuCann, Matthew Fisher, Les Lambert, Garry Nicholls, Phil Smee (of Strange Things Archives), Charlie Patton, Michelle & Gareth Taborn, Roland Clare, Terry Quirk, Dave Hallbery and Mick Fish from SAF.

Contents

Foreword

In the summer of 1964 a practically unknown British beat group calling themselves The Zombies released a single on Decca Records bearing the title "She's Not There". Incredibly dynamic and built on a driving, jazzy bass line over which drums, electric piano, guitar and voice were forming individual rhythms and patterns almost like those in a piece of Baroque chamber music, this unusual record gave a glimpse of a future where musical styles could be merged freely and without prejudice. It was very much of its time – a charming little slice of pop vinyl, easy to take, hard to let go.

Since the world at the time was practically delirious with Beatlemania, George Harrison's public praise became the final catalyst needed for this now-classic single to shoot to the top of the sales lists. The Americans particularly took to it, placing it at the Number 1 spot in the *Cashbox* Charts a month before Christmas that same year.

By then, however, problems had already started setting in for The Zombies. While their debut single had managed to reach Beatle-ish heights, the band was too inexperienced and under too much pressure to follow up the initial success. Equally importantly, they had no producer like The Beatles' George Martin to untangle their dreams and ideas for them, realise their true potential, home in on their individual personalities and turn it all into commercial success.

Despite these and other factors working against them, The Zombies produced a string of exceedingly interesting singles which have always fascinated devoted followers of the group as well as more general collectors of 1960s beat music. Moreover, as their swansong they released one of the best albums ever recorded by a rock group, the now-legendary *Odessey And Oracle*. Fittingly for a group of their name they returned to the Number 1 spot in the US singles charts with "Time Of The Season" in 1969, more than a year after they had ceased to exist.

By and large, this strange mixture of good and bad commercial luck probably benefited The Zombies. Unlike many other musicians from the 1960s rock scene, they all survived. And, like most quality artistic products, their music did too. In pop music particularly, facades and images have a tendency to crumble and fade with time. In a world that is finally learning to appreciate the voice of the 1970s Elvis Presley (instead of being blinded by political trends and images of bursting jump suits), and where Burt Bacharach is at last being recognised as a musical genius (and not a producer of supermarket Muzak), the combined talents of The Zombies have likewise managed to stand the test of time and even experience a second break-through. In fact, they are selling more records today than they did 35 years ago when they were still going as a group.

This is the first major Zombies biography to be published but, perhaps a little ironically, it concentrates on their story while they were still alive as a group. Other considerably shorter accounts of their history have delved deeper into the strange fate of their catalogue after the group disbanded, individual members' subsequent careers, and the short-lived reunions. I have found no need to repeat these sources, but have chosen to concentrate on the band's music at the time it was first written, performed and recorded. I'm sure every reader will have his own perception as to how the group's history and musical endeavours should be presented.

This is mine.

Claes Johansen,
Devon 2001

1

Greenbelt dreams

S t Albans, a mere twenty minutes north of London, has a history that goes all the way back to the Roman occupation, when it was founded under the name of Verulamium. The military constraints in the original planning, coupled with the fact that the town is built on a hill, means that its size, like other cities such as Oxford and Cambridge, is almost impossible to enlarge.

Consequently, there is perhaps a certain spirit of time-defying self-contentment over this area, which traditionally sets itself in opposition to neighbouring Watford, now practically a part of North London. More kinship is felt with Hatfield, only a stone's throw east of St Albans.

Unlike Luton to the north-west, which houses the large Vauxhall car factories, and Watford to the south-west with its breweries, St Albans is not a significant industrial town. However, for a long period in the middle of the twentieth century a vast number of people from the town and its surrounding villages would work at the local DeHavilland aircraft factory (later known as British Aerospace). Most famously, during the Second World War this company produced the Mosquito, a very light bomber, and later on, also manufactured the Comet, the first British jet passenger aeroplane.

In fact, three-fifths of the musicians who formed The Zombies were sons of fathers or mothers working for DeHavilland. It would appear the presence of this factory in the area worked as a further guarantee that even horrific events such as the 1939-45 war could not fully penetrate the greenbelt surrounding the town and its people. Though men were called up, many of them never went outside their immediate environment – they simply did their War Service by working for DeHavilland.

The increased activities at DeHavilland during the War also meant that a new workforce was arriving. That was how Colin Blunstone's father originally came to live in the area with his wife. After the War had ended, the family stayed on.

Born 24 June 1945 in Hatfield, Colin Edward Michael Blunstone was an only child. His mother was a housewife, while his father was employed as an aeronautical engineer at the aircraft factory. As was typical of the area's ambitious middle class, he made several attempts to break away from factory work and start up a business of his own. The choice of business came easy to him. As a young man he had been a hairdresser, so some five years after the War he bought his own shop and went back to hairdressing again. He kept the shop for a considerable period, then returned to the DeHavilland factory. When Colin grew a little older his mother went to work there as well.

The post-war years were generally meagre, so if the family

periodically found themselves short of means it did not appear to be anything other than that experienced by most people. Colin Blunstone still recalls the food rationing and the absence of central heating. For most of his younger childhood his parents never owned a car. Again, none of it seems to have mattered much, because there was another side to life which was perhaps more important than material welfare:

"We were a lot freer to do things than kids today," he told me, citing as an example how at the age of five or six, during the summer holidays, he and his friends would go out after breakfast, meet up, and be away from home playing all day. This was generally considered safe. There was a lot more open land around St Albans then than there is now, so it was very much a rural life. "In that sense I think that we were luckier than children are today, though looking back you realise that there were some hard times with regard to being a bit limited in what you had."

While discussing the lack of material wealth with Colin Blunstone, the issue immediately took him right to the heart of what he and many others consider a main problem in the history of The Zombies and how they appeared to the world.

"I know as a band we gave off that aura of being middle-class. In actual fact, maybe a couple of the guys' families were quite comfortable, but the others weren't. Because of where we came from we talk in a particular way. That's just what people speak like where we come from, and it sounded a bit like BBC accents. I think people made some judgements that weren't quite correct. My parents weren't wealthy at all. We may have been middle-class by aspiration but not by income."

Colin Blunstone has a strikingly varied view of his childhood and the society he grew up in. He is a person with a pronounced ability to see things from several sides. This makes him very pleasant company, and it evidently furnishes him with a quality of openness and vulnerability which became part and parcel of The Zombies' unique style. At the same time it also appears to have presented a problem for him in his artistic career. As a bit of a joke during my interviews, I sometimes suggested that the former Zombies members give their colleagues in the group titles according to the principle laid down in Roger Howgreaves' famous *Mister Men* children's book series. Everyone seemed to agree that Blunstone was *Mister Worry*.

Colin Blunstone's ability to see both sides of an argument at times made working with him a time-consuming process. However, it only made him all the more trustworthy as a first-hand witness to the times he grew up in and the significant events he has been part of.

With regards to naming any musical inspiration coming from his parents, he was completely dismissive. "There was no music at home," he simply said, though he also mentioned having many relatives, particularly on his mother's side, who played instruments, so times like Christmas would always be a true musical feast. Colin's mother had five brothers and three sisters, and all the men were members of a dance band. Furthermore, some of them were active players in a brass band. They nearly all mastered several instruments and sang as well, "beautiful harmonies." Being brought up within these surroundings, it was almost inevitable that Colin Blunstone would develop his singing voice and musical talent.

In the mid-fifties the BBC did not broadcast either rock 'n' roll or blues music. However, there was the famous Radio Luxembourg you could listen to if you were so inclined. At the age of ten Colin Blunstone got himself a radio, and from then onwards many of his nights were spent under the blankets, listening to this particular radio station's notoriously bad reception as it kept coming in and drifting off again.

A few years later he became the owner of a small record player and started buying records, his first single being Elvis Presley's "Heartbreak Hotel". From then on he was a devoted fan, not just of Presley but also of other contemporary rock pioneers such as Little Richard, Chuck Berry and Ricky Nelson. Presley's guitarist James Burton also made a big impression on him.

Paul Ashley Warren Atkinson was born 19 March 1946 in Cuffley. His father worked as an accountant for a stockbroker in the city of London. When Paul was nine years old the family moved to St Albans.

Like all other Zombies members, Atkinson mentions Elvis Presley's pre-army career as a huge influence. The very first record he bought was "Hound Dog", the next one "Don't Be Cruel". He then started to discover other artists such as Little Richard, whose "Lawdy Miss Clawdy" also became a prized item in his growing collection.

"I played it at home on my record player," he recalled. "My parents thought it was drivel. An absolute waste of time. They thought playing an instrument was a good idea, but they felt rock 'n' roll was a waste of time, as most parents did."

Brought up by considerably more musically-orientated parents, Rodney Terence Argent was born on 14 June 1945. His mother was one of eight children, most of whom still lived in St Albans, so throughout his childhood Argent had a substantial network of cousins, uncles and aunts spread around the town. Like Colin Blunstone's dad, Rod's father – Les Argent – was an aeronautical engineer at the DeHavilland factory, though it is doubtful that they knew each other more than by sight. In the evenings Les, who was a self-taught musician, worked as a semi-professional pianist. An active player for more than 60 years now, he has been the leader of two outfits performing jazz-tinged thirties and forties dance music – The Les Argent Quartet, and Les Argent and his Rhythm Kings.

Les didn't teach his son to play, but Rod Argent recalls how hearing his father play their upright piano around the house was an early influence on him. It all promoted the feeling that music was something natural to have around and to be engaged in.

Before Rod was ever taught anything musical he could quite easily and naturally play scales. He still recalls how in his mind he visualised the steps of the scale, and how he felt right from the beginning that this was all something extremely straightforward.

Apart from his father's playing, the first music Rod Argent recalls hearing was late nineteenth century romantic classical symphonies. This influence came via his mother, Molly, who was particularly fond of Tchaikovsky and Rachmaninov, interestingly composers who often put the piano to the fore. However, the first records Argent bought himself were by the famous Italian tenor, Mario Lanza.

From a very early age Rod Argent was eager to learn to play a musical instrument himself. Since he was obviously talented his parents bought him a harmonica when he was six years old. But it was the piano he was most keen on learning and since he was always messing around on the family's upright and kept begging to be taught, his parents eventually gave in and arranged for him to attend lessons locally. Their reluctance seems strange, unless it was economically founded; but in fact the idea turned out a failure. From the ages of seven to nine, when Rod Argent was taught the piano, he found himself spending less time at the instrument than at any other point in his life. It obviously didn't satisfy his creative mind to approach the instrument in the traditional, step-by-step manner.

For a closer description of Rod Argent as a friend and collaborator I approached Les Lambert, who from 1970 onward worked with him as a sound engineer for the post-Zombies group Argent:

"Rod is very cheerful," Lambert said. "He's not brought down by things. If you express any doubts about anything he'll look at you and go, 'What? Ah, come on. You can't be serious. No, that's not difficult.' Because he's prodigiously capable, Rod. Fantastic at almost anything he cares to do. It's frightening. He's very, very quick. He's got very good motor skills. His hands are quite 'arty', you see, he's got kind of double-jointed fingers. Normal people can cross their first and second finger. Well, he'll do the other two as well, and he can do them together, wrap all his fingers around each other. He is very intelligent too, and a nice guy, but the enthusiasm and the cheerfulness is what you notice, really."

The Zombies' bassist, Chris White, adds to this description that Rod Argent is a truly determined and focused artist, who is "always in a world of his own." This view seems to be confirmed by taking a look at photographs of the group all the way through their career. It has been said that there is always one member in every rock band who looks as though he stands out from the rest. You very much get this aura of aloofness with Rod Argent in almost every picture ever taken of the band, a mixture of body language and a certain determined gleam in the eye.

On the same shots White himself has more of a stoical air about him. Not surprisingly, guitarist Paul Atkinson describes him as "the daddy of the group". Not only the tallest of the five Zombies, Christopher Taylor White is also a full three years older than Atkinson, and two years older than the other three. He was born 7 March 1943 in Barnet,

North London, and is the only Zombie to have any rec-ollections of the Second World War and the bombing of London:

"I remember some of that, I also remember the End of the War Party, though I was only two. I can remember being my father's pet. I just remember that, really, because I was too young to really be conscious of what was going on."

White's great-uncle, a professor of mathematics, invented Pitman's method of teaching music, and in his spare time built large model steam trains from scratch for all the family's children to ride on. "So I suppose the family was crea-tive," Chris White stated, "but also there was this feeling that you do the best with your mind."

Professional musicianship found its way into the life of the Whites in a peculiar manner. Ted White, an uncle of Chris', was called up to be a soldier in the Second World War. How-ever, he was under the influence of his older brother, who had been an artillery officer in the First World War and con-vinced him that he should be a conscientious objector. Ted White was forced to go to court for his beliefs and eventu-ally ended up working in the Channel Islands. During the German occupation of the Islands in 1940, he was sent to a prison camp. It wasn't a luxurious life, to say the least, but nevertheless that was where he learned to play saxophone and joined his first band. After the War he took it up as a profession; he became an arranger for the BBC, a well-respected saxophone player and composer for the instru-ment.

Chris White's father, Harold, worked as a bus inspector for London Transport. This was a "reserved occupation", meaning that he was excluded from military service. He too was musically inclined and played double bass in an American-style dance band in the evening. "Mind you, they were all right until they heard the Glen Miller Band and all those things come over, because they were just knocked out," Chris White told me. "They'd never heard music like that and they just couldn't compete! I played ukulele as a child and my father played guitar. He used to sing songs like 'Frankie And Johnny' at family gatherings. So already then I started thinking in chord structures. We had a piano at home as well."

When Chris was five years old the White family moved from Barnet up to Markyate, a village just north of St Albans on the Bedfordshire border where, having left his position at London Transport, Harold opened up a general store.

For a description of Chris White as a person and as a musician I spoke to Procol Harum's Matthew Fisher, a longstanding fan of The Zombies who has occasionally worked with White as a fellow-songwriter and producer:

"Chris is a very flexible person," Fisher said. "He doesn't do things according to a set routine. He's very off-the-wall, very lateral thinking. He doesn't do things by numbers. I used to see myself as a pure musician-type, and Chris was much more 'arty' than me. I can't draw pictures or anything, but Chris is much more generally artistic than I am. He exposed me to that side of things and made me see things in a different way. It's the same thing I found working with David Bowie in the early seventies; he would say things that made me think, 'What?' It just didn't seem to be anything about music but it was the way he explained what he wanted. It was all weird terms like 'renaissance' or whatever. It was all a new experience to me, and Chris was like that too. He would talk in images rather than theoretical terms. As a person he is very laid-back, very easy-going. I really enjoyed working with Chris, it was great."

The son of a violin-playing father, Hugh Birch Grundy was born on 6 March 1945 in Winchester. Later the family moved to Hatfield and the father started working for

DeHavilland as an aircraft inspector while Hugh's mother was employed at the police headquarters in Welwyn Garden City as a co-ordinator.

All other members of The Zombies describe Hugh Grundy as being very into clothes and the way he looked. "I think we all were dress conscious," he commented. "I had a scooter. I think I was a bit of a Mod, you know – with the dangly bits on the handle bars!"

Judging by the way that The Zombies dressed and their tastes in music, it is easy to see Grundy's point. However, it doesn't appear that there was ever a real relationship between the band and the so-called Mod movement.

"I was never either a Mod or a Rocker," Rod Argent insists. "The main way it affected me was that for a while it was a bit unsafe to walk around the town in St Albans. There were two phases where things like that were going on. First there were the Teddy Boys when I was about eleven. That was dangerous, because they used to carry razors in their top pockets. Then that died down, and a bit later you had the Mods and Rockers thing. You just had to be careful. It was a bit dangerous for a while. You get these things with young males and hormones going mad and the male aggression having to find an outlet, and also the need for people generally to be part of a group and form their identity as part of that, though I never felt that way myself."

It is typical of the band members as a whole that their childhood and youth appear to have been free of what is now often seen as a natural and unavoidable rebellion against your parents. When I put this argument to Rod Argent he replied, "That is true, and it is certainly true of me. I think one of the reasons was that by the time I was sixteen The Zombies had started and immediately you were in a situation where you were a little bit of a celebrity. We had a following right from the start. Suddenly from the age of sixteen girls wanted to know you. So you didn't have to fight for your own identity to such an extent. You had an identity and you were somebody. You might have been a big fish in a very, very small pool, but at least you could create attention and your peer group thought you were cool and girls fancied you because you were in a band."

Chris White recalled some disagreements with his father over girlfriends, though nothing really serious – or as he put it himself, "That wasn't about music, and as long as I got my work done and passed my exams, fine. No, Dad always used to lend me the car. Never had any trouble, he was so easy-going. They were firm, it wasn't do-what-you-like, it was reasoned advice, and they never hit me. Look at your options, you know. And he'd be excited about things. So, yeah, I never had any problems at all."

"We were all fond of our parents," Hugh Grundy agreed. "They were very important to us. We listened to what they said. That was normal. I think the youth rebellion phenomenon is a sign of today as much as anything."

Not very rock 'n' roll, perhaps. On the other hand, Elvis Presley was very fond of his Mum and Dad too. And so is Paul Weller. Even Liam and Noel Gallagher talk openly of their devotion for their dear old mother. To cut a long story short, I doubt that parental relationships, social background, political views, looks, dress, age and occupation or, indeed, academic achievement can in any way predetermine whether or not you might be able to write and perform great music. What it might do, however, is add a certain direction and colouration to the kind of music you make.

2

The happiest days of your life

The emphasis that the press and The Zombies' own management put on the group's educational background, particularly at the time when they were starting to release records, was partly born out of necessity, since going to school was practically all the members had done career-wise before hitting the charts with their very first single. Then, as now, it was considered that all groups needed a strong image, which was normally developed by their managers or promoters by elaborating on features already present to some degree. Hence The Zombies were promoted as a band of intelligent successes and sometimes even intellectuals.

The issue is also otherwise important since, like it or not, going to school quite simply was the most significant thing that had happened in the group members' lives so far outside their families. I find it particularly noticeable that they all express great fondness for their years in primary school, while secondary education seems to have been a considerably more mixed pleasure. It may be that the predominant theme of longing for a more pure and uncomplicated phase in life, which can be found not just in The Zombies' lyrics but also in their whole mode of expression down to the very character of Colin Blunstone's voice and his way of using it could at least in part have a foundation in this particular, drastic change during a very sensitive stage of their personal development. If that sounds overdramatic, I suggest you read on now and judge later.

I'm sure that over the years quite a few non-British and younger generation followers of the group have been somewhat puzzled by descriptions of the members' educational background. The British school system was (and indeed still is) an intricate affair.

In the 1940s and 1950s, British children started school around the age of five, their following six years being spent at primary school until, often somewhat unprepared, they were faced with the decisive 11-plus exam. This test determined whether you were academically-inclined enough to go to Grammar School, which could give access to University, or if you were destined for a Secondary Modern School.

Considering that only some 10-15 percent of all British eleven-year-olds in the 1950s were allowed into the nation's Grammar Schools, it is sad to hear Chris White's laconic statement about the Secondary Modern School in St Albans:

"You were treated like a failure if you went there. They on the other hand would try to beat us up. It wasn't a good feeling. We were glad we hadn't gone for Comprehensives."

The White family were well aware of how important it was for young Chris to do well at this early point in his school-career. "In fact, my father's older brother was a very respected teacher," he told me. "So I went to the Grammar School because the alternative wasn't very palatable. I could have gone to a local Secondary School in the village, but I was determined to go to Grammar School because I'd heard that the initiation ceremony there was being thrown in a holly bush, and I didn't want any of that, or to be bullied."

The bullying aspect was particularly relevant to Chris, as he recalls, "I was purely on the art side. I hated sports. One thing was that I wore glasses, so if I took them off I couldn't see a damned thing, another that I was very fat up until the sixth form, where I suddenly lost a lot of weight."

Sometimes, pupils who had done well at the 11-plus exam were presented with a choice of several schools in their area to which they could apply. For boys, there were two schools in St Albans to choose between. First, there was the St Albans School, which was semi-private, meaning that it cost your parents money for you to go there, but it was possible to apply for a scholarship – that was the school Rod Argent, Paul Atkinson and Hugh Grundy went to. Second, there was the County Grammar School, which Chris White and Colin Blunstone attended. St Albans also housed a girls' Grammar School, where in fact The Zombies played some of their very first gigs (and I'm sure they enjoyed it very much).

Sixties beat connoisseur Phil Smee, these days a much-in-demand artist and the proprietor of Strange Things Archives, grew up just outside St Albans and went to one of the region's Secondary Modern Schools. To weigh things up I asked him for a view on the local school situation seen from the other angle.

"I know a lot of people who went through the education system at the same time as me," he said, "and I would say that a lot of those who went to Grammar Schools were pretty screwed up. They'd come out of the other end thinking that they were in some way superior, and it comes to them as a big shock that they are not being handed jobs on a plate and it doesn't unfold the way they thought it would."

While this characterisation doesn't seem to fit any of The Zombies members personally, it does perhaps explain why certain things went wrong for the group on the image front. The fact that they had between them 50 GCEs (General Certificate of Education examination passes) was not just mentioned in the press, it was hammered through every time the group appeared anywhere. As Colin Blunstone summed it up, "I think we antagonised a lot of people."

The St Albans Grammar School for Boys was a rather ordinary 1930s quadrangle building surrounding a yard with trees and bushes. The early years in schools of this kind presented a tough period for students in the British education system, and in fact they still do. Then it gets much easier. It may come as quite a surprise to people who have been faced with the comprehensive demands at an American High School or a North European "Gymnasium" that in Britain as soon as you had taken your "O" (Ordinary) levels – around the age of sixteen – you were pretty much capable of choosing your own subjects for the next exams, the "A" (Advanced) levels, taken around the age of eighteen, and that you needed to pass only two or three such exams to continue further up through the education system. Not all Grammar School students continued after "O" levels (Hugh Grundy didn't), but generally they were expected to.

"There were some nasty teachers at that school," Chris White told me. "However, there were some very nice ones too, particularly in the art department. I was always interested in painting and drawing."

Though Chris White describes St Albans Grammar School for Boys as a "pretty good education" it does appear that in some ways it was a rather dismal place. Particularly the head teacher probably wouldn't have scored many points in a popularity contest.

"He was quite a fearsome man called Ron Bradshore," White continued. "He used the cane a lot. Ridiculous. We never complained about it, but there was an edge of fear in it."

One of the students who would often feel the effects of Mr Bradshore's ideas on boys' upbringing was Colin Blunstone, two years White's junior at the school.

"It was a real ritual," he explained. "He used to like to make a little speech first. You didn't know at this point whether you'd be caned or not. You'd be in his study, and there used to be a lovely roaring fire, very different to the rest of the school. Then he'd wander around the room and you could hear him open this book cabinet where he kept his canes. He then took his cane out. This was all happening behind you. You could hear him swishing it, just to loosen his arm up. Swish, swish, swish. And then it would be, 'Bend over my desk, boy!' Then he would cane you. But the worst was afterwards. You would stand up, and then he would talk to you for two or three minutes. But you were on fire at this point, and you desperately wanted to go away, and your eyes were swelling up but you can't cry. That was the worst bit I remember. He would explain to you, 'Now, you understand why I've done this.' And of course he'd expect you to say, 'Yes, thank you sir' at the end of it."

While discipline appears to have been high on the school's agenda, music was not, at least not to begin with. Chris White recalled music lessons taught by a very old music master for half an hour a week learning the hymns for next week's assembly. Then, during White's last year, a young music teacher took over. Within a term he formed a school orchestra and a choir.

It was this new part of the environment that set the spark

and got White more actively interested in music. He had already been playing for a while – the family piano, the ukulele, acoustic guitar. Now, assisted by his father, he started practising more seriously for the double bass, which got him into the school band:

"My father's influence was 'keep it tight, keep the feel, a bass is a bass, it's the root of the whole thing.'"

For Colin Blunstone, years spent at primary school had already provided similar inspiration. His recollections from these early years in the education system form a strong contrast with his later experiences at grammar school:

"I felt very safe there. It was very much into the countryside. It was a wonderful school. The teachers there really tried to nurture their pupils and find the best in everyone. It was quite musical, singing and recorders and that sort of thing, though we didn't have an orchestra or anything like that. I did sing quite well as a young boy. I sang some solo songs at school concerts and in the classroom before my voice broke. So there was quite a bit of music in that school."

Blunstone's recollections of the musical environment during his early years at grammar school are as gloomy as Chris White's, if not worse. He had succeeded in getting his parents to buy him a cheap guitar and had got hold of a few books that would teach him how to play the basic chords. At this point, he had no intention of ever becoming a professional musician, it was just for fun. One day he took his guitar with him to school, and it was immediately confiscated.

Of course, in the mid-fifties bringing a guitar to school could be seen as the ultimate in youth rebellion. At this time strange and noisy records described as "rock 'n' roll" had started to hit the American charts, spearheaded by a certain loose-limbed truck driver from Memphis, Tennessee. The

worrying effect this new so-called musical style had on teenagers could be detected all the way over on the other side of
the Atlantic. In fact, some English kids were quite ecstatic –
among them Chris White:

"I can remember walking down the corridor the morning
after I'd heard 'Rock Around The Clock'. A wonderful feeling! That was such a dynamic record. After that it was 'Heartbreak Hotel' – and Lonnie Donnegan with 'Rock Island
Line'. Suddenly music started to take off a bit in my mind.
So we formed groups, skiffle groups."

Rod Argent's recollections of the 11-plus exam and what
followed are marked by his typically straight-forward and
constructive manner of addressing a problem:

"I just remember thinking, 'Well, I got to have a go at this,'
and I was really pleased when I managed to get the scholarship. I put down St Albans School as my first choice, and
I put the grammar school down as my second. I was just
fortunate to get the first choice."

Again, I consulted Phil Smee for a different angle on the
issue. "I didn't go to St Alban's School myself," he told me,
"but we used to see the people who went there and they
were scared out of their wits. Apart from everything else, the
place looks like a castle, because it is part of the Abbey building. It's changed now, but it really wasn't an education to be
sought after."

At institutions such as the Grammar School and St Albans
School, students in those days were normally expected to fall
into one of three main groups – there were the technically
inclined, the artistically inclined, and the sports fanatics. It
appears that the reason why Colin Blunstone and Chris
White knew only little of each other during their school
days had less to do with the age difference than with the fact
that Blunstone was known as a sports person, while Chris
White was 100 percent artist (I could be mistaken, but it

sometimes felt to me during my interviews with both of them that even today this distinction somehow plays a part in their relationship). Over at St Albans School, Rod Argent found it considerably more difficult to conform to such standards.

"I didn't belong in any of those groups," he told me. "I was a pretty good little footballer, and yet I also loved music. They couldn't take that on board. My headmaster at the private school could never work me out at all. In some ways he looked at me as being a rebel because I wore my hair long and I used to wear slightly pointed shoes – you didn't have to do much to be a rebel at that school, I tell you! For other people this was enough to make him go into a rage, pick them up by their lapels and go completely over the top. But on the other hand he also saw me singing in the cathedral choir and being very good at it too. He just couldn't work it out at all. He was very puzzled by me."

However, in Argent's early years at St Albans School it wasn't music or sport that he did best in, it was English. He recalls being fascinated by romantic poets such as Keats and Shelley. Shakespeare also made a big impact – "The language spoke to me; it had an indefinable, spiritual quality."

Considerably more daring was their teacher's introducing them to Henry Miller's novels, *The Tropic Of Cancer* and *The Tropic of Capricorn*. "At the time that was really subversive," Argent told me. "I loved Henry Miller's writing for its energy, momentum and all-encompassing taking everything in. I loved the combination of spirituality with complete acceptance of any earthiness and anything sexual. Incidentally, this master was the same guy that Stephen Hawking said inspired him at the same school. He was a couple of years ahead of me."

Like Chris White, Argent vividly recalls hearing for the first time "Rock Around The Clock". His cousin, Jim Rodford, lived at the bottom of the road where Rod lived with his parents and his younger sister. Jim had two sisters and, like Rod, was a musical lad. When he was fourteen he already played in a skiffle group called The Bluetones, often referred to as the first modern music group in the whole of the St Albans area.

One day when Rod went down to visit his cousin, he found Jim's sisters busy playing their records by Bill Haley, who at that point had just started to become popular in Britain. "I heard the first couple of things they were playing and I thought, 'Ah! This is horrible! I hate this!' But I stayed there, and after a couple of hours I was just completely hooked. That's what turned me on to rock 'n' roll."

Soon afterwards Rod discovered Elvis Presley through such future classics as "Hound Dog" and "Don't Be Cruel". Not only does he recall that the experience completely changed his idea of music at the time, he also to this day maintains that "Presley was transcendent", though his appreciation remains oriented around the first three years of Elvis' career.

For a while Argent found himself not wanting to bother with any other music except all the rawest rock 'n' roll he could lay his hands on. Then he discovered another musical form which would have an equally important influence on his own style later on. He heard Miles Davis for the first time on the groundbreaking album *Milestones*, and it immediately captivated him.

Meanwhile, admiration for classical music remained. Working in close collaboration with the local Abbey, St Albans School had a choir of which young Argent was a long-standing member. He had already learned the mechanics of reading music through the two years of piano lessons he had attended, and in the choir there was a lot of "sight reading" (singing straight from the sheet music without preparation). It was a considerable commitment. Wednesday was their day off, but apart from that there were rehearsals twice a day. As a consequence, by the time Argent finally left the choir his sight reading and singing were tremendously strong.

I asked Rod Argent to what extent the Impressionist composers also had an influence on him. There does seem to be an element of this genre in some of his own compositions.

"I don't think I got to know Delius until I was about probably seventeen or eighteen," he replied. "So that was a few years later. Then I heard him and liked him. Debussy I was always aware of, but he wasn't my favourite. Bartok knocked me out completely, and Stravinsky. But at the same time I loved Bach, and I've never stopped loving Bach as well. That was great, too. I remember we used to sing the 'Matthew Passion' by Bach with an orchestra, and that was just sublime. That was fantastic."

Over the years much emphasis has been put on Rod Argent's background in choir singing, and for good reasons. The confidence and style of The Zombies' vocal harmony work draw a straight line back to this early part of his life. There is little doubt that St Albans School had a very good choir, which taught its members well. Responsible for all this was the organist, Peter Hurford, who is still today highly regarded as an organist. Hurford also brought a lot of modern classical music into the repertoire, and being very young and impressionable Rod Argent immediately took to it.

Like the grammar school (today Verulam School), St Albans School is still operating as a reputable, well-functioning educational institution. With some of Chris White and Colin Blunstone's less flattering recollections in mind, it must be emphasized that these events took place more than forty years ago and have nothing whatsoever to do with the way either of the schools is run today.

St Albans School goes back more than a thousand years as

a building and has functioned as a school for centuries. It was previously a boarding school, but around the time when Rod Argent, Hugh Grundy and Paul Arnold started attending, several things were changing. Boarding was finishing, so all new students were "day boys". Likewise, some of the customs that typified boarding schools were in the process of being phased out.

While things were fine on the musical front there were other aspects of life at St Albans School which both Rod Argent and Hugh Grundy felt considerably less keen on. "Some of the teachers were a bit crazy, I think," said Grundy. "We got our own back by parking their bubble-cars up against the brick wall so they couldn't get in the front door and things like that."

As in the case of the grammar school, physical punishment was not only common, but was sometimes allegedly taken to a degree where it seems to have ceased being a means of maintaining discipline and veered towards sheer perversion.

"The masters were allowed to practise corporal punishment," Rod Argent recalled. "In fact I had a period in my second year where I had a form-master who saw how well I did in English and that I was good at music, and he couldn't understand why I was so bad at physics. So he used to beat me every week. Every week. I soon learned that he had homosexual tendencies as well. I had to go into his room and I had to pull my pants down and he would beat me with his slipper. I never told my parents, and I don't know why. I still don't know why. I just didn't want to upset the apple cart. I really wish I had done, because they would have gone crazy. They would have gone absolutely bananas."

Unsurprisingly, Rod Argent found that he did very badly academically for the first few years at the school. "In English I usually came top of the whole year, but in everything else

I came bottom, not just of the 33 people in the class, but of the whole year."

Typically for the spirit in the Argent home this situation doesn't appear to have resulted in any undue pressure from Rod's parents. A few years later, when he reached Upper School and could chose subjects more to his own liking, he started doing considerably better, and eventually came out with truly excellent results.

Hugh Grundy was in the same class as Rod Argent and was likewise musically interested (unlike Argent, Grundy had achieved "common entrance" to the school, meaning that his parents paid for him to go there). His life as an active musician started one day when he decided to join the school band. This decision was partly born out of convenience. At St Albans School, Fridays were known as "School Corps Day", meaning that on this day all the boys would have to go to school dressed in army uniforms and either parade or be chased around the landscape like conscripts. The only exceptions were the members of the band, which consisted of drums and bugles, who seemed to live a considerably more peaceful existence.

"It appeared to me that all they ever did was go down the band hut and clean their gear and go out on parade whenever necessary," Grundy told me. "I thought, 'I'd like some of that!'"

So Hugh Grundy applied and was accepted to join the school band. He started as a bugle player, a job he managed quite well. Unfortunately, when they went out on parade the bugle players would always be in the back of the band. If you paraded through town, there was little chance that the girls might see you down there, and even if they did all they'd see was a red and swollen face blowing into a small horn instrument. "I thought to myself, 'The drummers are up front, and they don't have to blow these bugles so hard and contort their faces and all that. I need to get up to the front and play those drums, because that looks more fun to me.' Not to forget, of course, that rock 'n' roll music was beginning to come in, and although my father was keen on playing the violin and wished me to do the same, I thought, 'Maybe it should be the guitar – or the drums even!'"

Grundy asked to be moved over and play drums instead, which again was agreed. He soon discovered that he had a natural aptitude for the instrument, but more importantly he now found himself at the front of the band.

"It was at that point Rod said to me, 'We're forming a band.' So that's when we started."

3

D.I.Y. musicians

By the time Rod Argent asked Hugh Grundy to form a band, he had already been rehearsing for a while with guitarist Paul Atkinson. Atkinson had a brother two years older, and it was because of him that the family had moved to the area since he had been accepted at the prestigious St Albans School.

Around this time Paul's father gave him a recorder for his tenth birthday. Paul taught himself to read music and then graduated from the recorder to a violin, which his mother bought him when he was twelve. He had violin lessons but hated them because, though he liked the instrument, he simply found it too difficult to play. When Paul had finished Primary School he also started going to St Albans School, and after a couple of years there he started going to a Music Club that was held after school hours.

The Music Club met every Tuesday in a small classroom,

and all students from the school were invited to come along and bring an instrument. The environment appears to have been surprisingly "free-form"; there wasn't even a teacher in charge of things.

"There was a guy that I met there who had a guitar," Atkinson told me. "He was interested in my violin and after a brief chat we agreed to switch. So I came home with a guitar, much to my mother's disgust because it was quite a crappy old guitar and it was quite a nice violin. Anyway, that was what I wanted to play."

By now the skiffle craze was starting in England and the undisputed king of the movement, Lonnie Donegan, quickly became Paul Atkinson's hero. A little later he got even more hooked on Chet Atkins, buying every record released, and starting to teach himself to play the guitar. After driving his parents crazy with the same three chords, Paul eventually started taking real guitar lessons, which he continued over the next eighteen months. During that time he still went to the Music Club on Tuesdays.

"One day, when I was about fourteen, there was this guy banging away on a piano," Atkinson recalled. "He was pretty good, actually. I was sort of joining in with him on guitar and he said, 'Do you want to start a group?' It was Rod."

With the aid of Hugh Grundy they soon began rehearsing as a trio at the Music Club meetings and also gave a few informal performances during late 1961 and early 1962. This trio, which apparently didn't have a name, was in fact the very first version of what would soon develop into The Zombies.

"There weren't that many groups around St Albans, so the fact that we had a band was quite a noteworthy thing," recalled Paul Atkinson. "I don't remember there being any other bands coming out of St Albans School at that time."

One of the many problems with forming groups in those

days was obtaining decent instruments to play on. Way into The Zombies' semi-professional career they would still be playing on extremely primitive equipment. Rod Argent had to rely on poorly amplified acoustic pianos, while Hugh Grundy started out with just a snare drum and a cymbal or two, then slowly built up his kit in ways that wouldn't involve too much of an economic investment. "I used to sneak down the band hut and 'borrow' a couple of drums when we practised after school hours," he admitted.

In an equally unorthodox manner Paul Atkinson helped a friend of Rod Argent build a bass guitar, intending to join the group. The friend's name was Paul Arnold.

Atkinson's father had a small workshop in the back garden with a workbench and a vast number of tools. One day Arnold arrived at the guitarist's house with a hunk of wood and a collection of bass guitar parts which he had bought. They had also managed to borrow a real bass, on which they modelled their own instrument.

"We cut it out as a solid body bass," Atkinson said. "It was pretty primitive but it worked. We measured this other bass and had to get the fretboard and everything right – that was tricky! It took us a few weeks, but we did it. It didn't stay in tune very well, but it worked for our early purposes."

Shortly before Paul Arnold joined the group he came up with an idea. One of his classmates over at the grammar school played guitar and had been talking of forming a group as well. Would it be an idea to propose him to come along as well?

Why not, replied the others and asked for the name of this guitarist. And being a grammar school boy, Arnold replied not by telling them the first name of the person in question, but by referring to him by surname instead.

"It's Blunstone," he said.

4

Congregation of the living dead

Over at St Albans Grammar School, Colin Blunstone was a popular character. However, it wasn't for his musical abilities that he was most renowned. "You knew Blunstone," Chris White told me. "He was quite good-looking and a good sportsman, but I had no idea that he could sing and play guitar."

One person at the school who knew Colin Blunstone better than most was his friend and classmate Paul Arnold. In fact, since the students were placed in alphabetical order in the classroom, Blunstone was sitting right behind Arnold. One day Paul turned around and said, "I've got this friend who wants to start a band." He knew that Blunstone had a guitar and they had talked about bands before. So he continued, "What do you think – do you want to be in it?"

Colin immediately answered yes, though in truth he was wondering what he had got himself into. He wasn't sure whether he was good enough to be in a band or not. Even more importantly, he had no urge to become a real musician, and the idea of being a lead singer was not in question at this point. However, he had been bragging to Arnold about wanting to be in a band, and now that the chance had arrived it was difficult to chicken out.

Taking the step and becoming a real group was just as much of a challenge for the other four people involved. Paul Arnold had been playing a bit of guitar for a while and rehearsing on his new bass, but it was the first time he was to join in with the rest of the band. Rod Argent, Paul Atkinson and Hugh Grundy on the other hand were stepping out of the Music Club environment for good. Luckily, Rod's cousin Jim was there to aid the transition.

This relationship between Rod Argent and Jim Rodford is at the heart of The Zombies' career and most of Rod Argent's subsequent endeavours as well (Jim Rodford was the bass player in the 1970s group Argent). To find out more about the nature of this friendship I once again turned to Les Lambert whose recollection, albeit from a later stage, seems to sum up the situation in general:

"Jim Rodford was quite protective of Rod, even though he didn't need it," Lambert said. "Jim admired him. Jim was older, three years, but it seemed like it was more. They got on really well but Rod was always kind of the golden boy. Jim's a very good musician, but Rod was the star, no question."

Since Rodford had been playing in the popular local St Albans band The Bluetones for several years, he kindly proposed that Rod Argent and his friends could hold their first rehearsal at the place where his own band practised at that time, a small youth club called The Pioneer Club. He even let them use The Bluetones' top notch-equipment and set it all up for the occasion. Furthermore, since it was the first time Hugh Grundy got acquainted with a real drum kit, Rodford gave him a few lessons in hand-and-foot co-ordination before the group started rehearsing for real. Typically, Grundy's natural talent and positive attitude made it easy for him to master the principles quickly. Then the other players started to arrive.

"I met Colin for the first time at this bus stop in St Albans," Paul Atkinson recalled. "I was standing there in my raincoat with my guitar. It was drizzling. He got off the bus and we walked down the street to this club to do our rehearsal. He looked like a rough guy. He looked a bit dubious, and he was really recruited as a guitar player, so he brought his guitar along."

This statement may come as a surprise to anyone who has ever met or seen Colin Blunstone, one of the least "rough-looking" people you could possibly come across. This particular occasion, however, was a bit unusual. Blunstone had been playing Rugby on the Wednesday before. "Someone's head had gone into my face and well and truly flattened my nose. Furthermore, I had two black eyes and a lot of strapping across my face. I think they were all a bit apprehensive when I turned up," he told me.

Colin Blunstone also recalled that first meeting in the late spring of 1962 as being dedicated entirely to rehearsing a traditional instrumental song called "Malaguena". This song had probably been suggested by Rod Argent since, throughout the group's career, he was their undisputed leader. Blunstone, on the other hand, obediently got on with his rhythm guitar playing and soon found that there had been no cause for his concerns about joining a group.

"It was only two chords," he told me. "We played it all morning. I just went from A-minor to E-minor. I thought, 'This is quite easy.' Rod was going to be the singer, but he didn't sing that day. There was an old broken down piano in the corner, and he went over there and started playing 'Nut Rocker' by B. Bumble & the Stingers [a UK hit in late April 1962]. I just remember thinking, 'We've got this guy who's going to be the singer, and he's a bloody genius keyboard player. Surely, he should be more incorporated in this.'"

Colin Blunstone's feeling that there was something wrong with the balance in the group was completely true. However, putting more emphasis on Argent's keyboard playing was but one feature that had to be worked on. Right from the start there was a feeling that perhaps Paul Arnold wasn't committed enough.

"Paul Arnold was kind of quiet," Paul Atkinson told me. "He wasn't terribly dedicated. He liked the idea of being in a group, and he liked playing bass, but to be honest Paul was a little lazy. He didn't like to rehearse very much."

Nevertheless, during his relatively brief time with the group Paul Arnold came up with two important ideas which became crucial for the group's future. First, there was the suggestion that Colin Blunstone should be included in the line-up. Second, it was Arnold who finally managed to find an acceptable name.

For a while the group had called themselves names like The Sundowners, which they took from a popular Western movie of the time. They were also briefly The Mustangs, as well as a few less serious names such as Fred Grease and the Axles or Chatterley and the Gamekeepers. Then Arnold finally suggested The Zombies.

"We thought that with such a weird, bizarre name nobody else would think of it," Paul Atkinson stated. "That was one of the criteria – it had to be a name that nobody else could possibly have thought of. This one certainly fitted that requirement, so we stuck with it."

In the beginning, around half of the songs the group played were instrumentals, and for several months Blunstone remained rhythm guitarist. "We did a lot of Shadows tracks," he recalled. "I think we also tried to get a bit of a 'Shadows walk' going as well, but we had a few accidents doing that. We did 'Shaking All Over', and we tried to get a routine going for that too. There were a lot of guitars swivelling around and all that. By then I was the singer in the band and I remember jumping up at one point, probably when I shouldn't have, and I nearly had my head chopped off by a swivelling guitar. So we thought we'd better knock that on the head because the choreography wasn't all that good. But we used to play the current music of the time, really."

In the meantime Hugh Grundy was getting more and more familiar with playing his rudimentary drum kit:

"It came sort of naturally," he explained. "I picked up one or two ideas from the boys in the band. I also used to listen to Radio Luxembourg and the BBC Light Programme when it was beginning to get into rock 'n' roll slowly. It was really interesting to me, so I used to listen very, very carefully and analyse it and think, 'All right, I can do that,' and drive my mum and dad crazy at the dinner table practising with knives and fork on the table."

No one seems to remember exactly when it was decided that Colin Blunstone should take over from Rod Argent as lead singer. "I think they were only trying to stop me playing the guitar," Blunstone humbly suggests. "I don't know what else it could be, because they'd never heard me sing."

Others recall it differently. According to Paul Atkinson, "As soon as we heard Colin sing we went, 'Wow, you've got a great voice!' So it was agreed that Colin should be the singer, and he gave up the guitar."

Rehearsing at the Pioneer Club had been a one-off event. The band soon had to find their own places to meet and practise. "We shuffled around quite a bit between St Albans and Hatfield, like church halls or whatever," Paul Atkinson told me.

Paul Arnold's departure from the group had been on the cards for some time, but one particular episode appears to have been the proverbial straw that broke the camel's back.

"It was very cold, and some of these places we were rehearsing in had no heat in the winter," recalled Paul Atkinson. "We would play and play and play just to keep ourselves warm. I think we were playing 'Peggy Sue' by Buddy Holly, which has basically three chords – A, D and E. You can play open strings for that on a bass, and that was exactly what Paul was doing. We caught him with his left hand in his pocket, because he was cold. He was trying to keep it warm. We said, 'Come on. You can do better than that.' But all in all, we felt it was time for a more accomplished musician. He didn't seem surprised. It was kind of mutual. He was getting ready to go off to college, because he was going to be a doctor and he had to move to Scotland to go to university. He would have had to leave the band anyway, so it wasn't too dramatic."

The remaining group now started looking for someone to replace Paul Arnold. They didn't have to search very long. Paul Arnold's older brother, Terry, had gone to school with Chris White and they were still friends, so a line of communication was already established. White also knew Rod Argent, whom he had previously approached with the view of Rod joining a dance band Chris was leading. "Someone said he was a keyboard player," Chris White told me, "so we actually met two years before we got together. But he wasn't interested."

This particular meeting had happened shortly after White had left St Albans Grammar School and started attending art school. "I didn't necessarily want to go to university," he told me. "In fact, in those days it was quite a difficult thing to do. But I was always good at drawing, so I decided to concentrate on that. I was going to be an art teacher. So I thought going to art college would be the best thing. I got all my "O" levels, I got about eight out of nine, and decided all I need is really an "A" level in art. So I just did it in one year instead of the usual two and then went to art school. It must have been in 1960. I loved art school, but I didn't realise it was going to be the hotbed for English rock and roll. In fact, I think the art schools of that period were some of the best creative forces in this society. It was so inventive. It was also the sixties. We were coming out of the War's rationing and everything, and so invention was the key thing. Plus at art school there were 75 girls to 25 boys. And coming straight from an all-boys school the first lesson I had in there was sculpture with a nude female model! So it was very good, and they used to have great dances and that's where we came across a lot of modern jazz, Miles Davis and everything. They had very good school plays every year, Shakespeare and Shaw and everything, so I used to do a lot of stage-managing and property managing and help with the scenery and help with the organisation side. I also read a lot. It was a great, creative time. I was very happy at art school."

Unlike the rest of the group, Hugh Grundy had by now left the education system altogether and taken up work in a bank. "With the amount of 'O' levels I had it seemed like a good thing to do," he recalled. "I never reached 'A' levels. I'm sure my parents would have liked me to, but at the time banking seemed like a good idea. That's what the plan was, but of course the group thing came along."

Around late 1962 The Zombies had started playing some low-key gigs, gradually reaching a level where they could call themselves semi-professional in the sense that they were sometimes paid money for their performances. Others might find a problem with pinning even such a humble title on any group with four instruments, a lead singer and two backing vocalists all playing and singing through what Chris White recalls as "two crappy little amps".

Obviously, going from The Bluetones' first-class equipment at the very first rehearsal to a situation such as this had been a pretty depressing experience. Nevertheless, the group carried on enthusiastically, now practising mainly in yet another tin-roofed hut by the name of Hatfield Youth Club. This location was particularly convenient for drummer Hugh Grundy, who was going out with a girl living next door to the club.

"She was the organist's daughter," he confirmed. "I used to pop in there while the others were working on arrangements and things. I said, 'I'm just going to disappear and see my girlfriend.' It was so close, so why not?"

Chris White also remembers Grundy's sudden disappearances:

"Every time we took a break during the numbers, he'd nip off to see her. He always disappeared when we were talking or anything. At one of the first gigs he came up to Colin and said, 'What's the name of our bass player?' We'd been rehearsing for all this time, but he'd never spoken to me because he was off with this girlfriend."

5

Live Zombies

By and large, the music that The Zombies were playing during this early stage consisted predominantly of what Paul Atkinson confessed were, "Shadows numbers and other lame instrumentals." That was very much what audiences of the day demanded. The band's own preferences remained more eclectic.

"Trad jazz appealed to me, very much so," recalled Chris White, "because it was such good fun to dance to. One of my other influences were the old songwriters, like Rogers & Hammerstein and Cole Porter. My family loved me getting into rock 'n' roll, because they were great music lovers. In fact, to buy equipment my daddy lent us money. Well, he'd go and buy equipment and we'd pay it back out of the gigs. He was very generous in supporting us."

White's recollections support the view that by the early sixties the British parent generation and society in general had become much less hostile towards rock 'n' roll than they had been five or six years earlier, when the first Presley and Bill Haley records had come out.

Perhaps it also helped that the genre seemed to have adapted a new name in Britain, which made it more acceptable and less associated with Teddy Boys and leather-clad bikers – it was now known as rhythm 'n' blues. For the first year or so of The Zombies' career they very conveniently added the abbreviation "R&B" to their name, and though "Zombies R&B" indeed looks like an odd juxtaposition it at least gave them some street credibility. Ironically, the style of music they and many of their contemporaries branded rhythm 'n' blues wasn't quite what it was supposed to be. R&B had started out as a term mainly for black American vocal groups and jazzy blues combos. However, in early '60s Britain it became a synonym for what well-known jazz musician Kenny Ball (in Alan Clayson's book *Beat Merchants*) wittily discards as "rock 'n' roll with a mouth organ".

The important thing, however, was that camouflaged behind this new name, rock 'n' roll was again considered to be a very fresh and interesting form of music. In reality, what happened was that young musicians who had previously been playing skiffle suddenly came to a point in their lives where they could afford to buy real instruments and amplifiers – and skiffle played on such equipment is pretty close to rock 'n' roll.

This transition is very much what happened for Chris White, and also for the Argent-Grundy-Atkinson trio when they moved out of St Albans School's Music Club and into the town's gigging circuit. Likewise, the manner in which they gained acceptance in their parents' eyes seems to follow the rule book at the time – and a positive attitude from your parents was important when you lived at home and depended on their support, not just financially but also for transport and, indeed, a place to rehearse.

"We used to rehearse around my house and make a complete racket in the dining room," Rod Argent told me. "The bloke next door was on night work and he must have been kept awake all day long, but he never complained. My mother was in her early forties around the time when the Zombies started, but she loved the music we played."

The trad jazz revival around 1961 saw young Argent hitting the pubs of St Albans several nights at week. "It was a social thing," he now reckons, "but I also used to like the whole feeling of the beat-type people who used to go to those places. I would never have counted myself as a beatnik, but I did love the music."

One of Argent's idols at this time was Duke Ellington, whose music he had heard for the first time in one of these jazz clubs. Otherwise, as far as jazz was concerned the people who fascinated him deeply even at a very young age were, apart from the aforementioned Miles Davis, saxophonists John Coltrane and Cannonball Adderly, and the pianist Bill Evans. The more populist jazz musicians of the day impressed him less. "Brubeck never really spoke to me at all. I always enjoyed Oscar Peterson, he's the most wonderful player with the most fantastic technique, but he never spoke to me. With the others, it was the intensity I liked. The more fiery, the more intense – that was really what spoke to me."

The optimistic DIY mentality of skiffle also had an impact on Rod's taste in music. He admits to feeling a slight hero-worship for his cousin Jim. "I went to see him for the first time when I was about eleven and he was fifteen. I was completely starstruck. I thought, 'I want to do that, and I don't care if I'm inaudible and just playing chords all night.'"

As with some of the other Zombies members, Rod Argent

recalls being impressed with the King of Skiffle, Lonnie Donnegan, but the real rockers always stayed closest to his heart. "I loved Buddy Holly, but I liked Elvis more, because he seemed more raw to me and more black."

Likewise, Colin Blunstone's preferences included the classic early rockers, but he was less keen on some of their British counterparts. "I didn't particularly like skiffle except when it first came out," he told me. "I was still into rock 'n' roll in '60-'61. At the time, classical music didn't appeal to me. It was just purely rock 'n' roll I was interested in. I love classical music now, but at the time I didn't think that was quite me. We were into Cliff Richard and the Shadows, as I remember. And also I did like trad jazz.

"All the band members used to go to local jazz clubs together. There was the Hatfield Jazz Club in the Red Lion in Hatfield. That's a pub, and that was on a Monday night. They just had a great atmosphere, these places. I liked the music very much. It wasn't overpoweringly loud so it meant you could meet your friends and talk. St Albans Jazz Club was on a Wednesday night, but I think Hatfield was my favourite one. Every night of the week you could probably go to a jazz club."

From late 1962 onwards The Zombies started playing more and more gigs locally in the St Albans area. Chris White:

"The first jobs we played with the Zombies were great, 'cause we thought we were fantastic. My first bass was home built, not by myself though, I got it from somebody else. In those days you couldn't afford to buy instruments. I think the main problem nowadays is there are no places for bands to play. We could at least get a few quid a week playing. There were lots of youth places to play – not any more. It's all centred on records now, and the problem is that the kids don't get the chance to learn to play to an audience.

Mostly people go into the studio with an enormous amount of money, with a very experienced engineer and producer, and produce something fantastic, but they get no idea of how to perform it. In fact, all they're concerned about is that is sounds the same on stage. It's that craft of being able to entertain that I'm beginning to miss."

Colin Blunstone added, "When I think back I don't know how on earth we did it. If we were lucky, someone's parents would help get us there. Later on Hugh got a car, and he used to give me a lift. Before he had a car he had a scooter, and I swear that on occasions we got him, his drums, me *and* a guitar on that scooter. I know it sounds unlikely, and he didn't have a big drum kit, but I'm sure we did [all other group members confirm this; in fact they seem unlikely ever to forget the sight]. Sometimes we'd take all our gear and we'd go on the bus. That was in the very early days; we'd just get there any way we could. Later on Chris could borrow his dad's car, because he was a bit older than us. Sometimes we played for nothing, but we tried to get £6 a night. That would be £5 to reinvest in equipment, and £1 for travelling expenses. I don't think we ever got much more than that when we were amateurs."

One rock fan who was particularly well acquainted with the gigging situation around St Albans was Phil Smee:

"The places in St Albans where bands could play were often called 'halls'. Some are still there, some are not. Mostly they were just big huts. Some of them had kitchens and toilets, so they would have been church halls. They were affiliated to a nearby church, and you used to have functions in them all the time – weddings and so on. They always had a quite high stage at one end with curtains and everything. They were dotted all around St Albans. The gigs that would be advertised were cheap to get into. Often there were no drinks available, you would just go in. Some of the gigs were to do with Rugby clubs. They would play the weekend dance."

One place in particular where The Zombies R&B were frequently invited to appear was the Old Verulamians' Rugby Club, where Colin Blunstone was a member.

"I would have loved to have played first-class Rugby," he told me. "In all honesty I wasn't good enough, but I did love playing. Anyway, they used to have a dance band there, and they would have about six couples dancing to this dance band in the evening. No one was interested. I heard that some friends of mine played a little bit of rock 'n' roll in the interval. They were very keen, but I knew that we were a bit better. I thought, 'I'll get our band in here.' So we played, and the first time there were probably twenty people in there. The next time we played there was around 70. Before we knew where we were they had to put a huge extension, like a tent, on to the Rugby club because they couldn't get all the people in. Then we started playing at other Rugby clubs. That was quite a step forward for us. Instead of playing in very small places, we were playing to 2-300 people."

Another major step forward was a gig the band played at St Albans Town Hall on May 27, where a local promoter was present to evaluate if they were good enough to take on an evening at the local Ballito's factory, a much bigger venue. The occasion is recalled with rather mixed emotions. For a start, no audience turned up so the groups were playing to an empty hall. The Zombies opened, but the top act were The Crestas (a Sheffield band who later went on to record one solitary single for Fontana, "To Be Loved", in 1965).

Colin Blunstone: "They were very, very good. For one reason or another they didn't have hit records, but believe me they were great. We were completely in awe of them. We were sharing a dressing room with them. We just used to amble up and play gigs, but when they arrived they took their clothes off and changed them, and in particular they took their stage shoes out and polished them. I was so impressed!"

During The Zombies' spot they suffered a small accident that had never happened to them before – Paul Atkinson broke a string. "We didn't know what to do," Blunstone continues. "We had twenty minutes, maybe half an hour spot to fill. About twelve or thirteen minutes out of that was taken up by Paul finding a string and all the rest of it. To cap it all Rod had lost his voice as well. We did that Beatles song 'From Me To You' and Jim had to walk across the hall and lean over and sing the falsetto part into Rod's microphone. It was a bit of a disaster that night. I don't know how, but we did actually play and we passed the audition. I think that Jim Rodford put in a good word for us."

Whatever the case may be, The Zombies found themselves playing Ballito's less than a month later.

"That was the first place I remember seeing them," recalled Phil Smee. "It's not there any more, but it was a big place that made women's stockings. It was just outside St Albans on the way to Hatfield. It was a very old-fashioned, Victorian building – high walls and big windows. It covered a very big area. Ballito's had a very big main hall, which was really a canteen for the workers. It was a vast place where they used to have boxing most of the time. When groups were there they would play this great big hall. They used to play the Saturday dance there. It was quite old-fashioned. Boys and girls would sit either side, and some would dance in the middle. Very basic, not like a concert at all. Half the time you would be hanging around the bar trying to get a drink, but you weren't old enough. Horrible Mods and Rockers strutting around. These places were very dangerous to be in sometimes! In a way it spoiled the atmosphere. Virtually every week a fight would break out, particularly in the bar – quite nasty fights. So being quite young as I was, around fourteen-fifteen, I used to keep well away from it."

The records kept by Paul Atkinson – the band's "treasurer" at the time – list mainly youth clubs and schools throughout 1963, along with quite a few local "halls". The actual number of these engagements, however, was bigger than suggested in the records, since quite a few of them were non-profitable and hence not chronicled.

"Sometimes they played the Faulkner Hall or The Pioneer Youth Club," Phil Smee continued. "Those were tiny, tiny places. Probably built in the late fifties, they were single-storey buildings, quite low. Reminded me of kindergarten type of schools, with notice boards and battered old ping-pong tables. It cost very little to get in, like two shillings and sixpence. The Market Hall was a place where, on Wednesdays, they used to sell cattle. On Saturday evenings when you went there you could still smell the cattle. It was a funny place. They used to book a lot of R&B acts there, so you got The Pretty Things and bands like that. A queue used to form down an alleyway next to the Market Hall which went out into the main road, a long snaking queue, but when you got inside it was only this great big hall made of wood and bricks with tin rafters. You went in through a tiny little door at one end, and to the left were the boys' toilets and to the right were the girls' toilets, and that was it, you were into the hall, just one great big place with a stage at the end."

By the summer of 1963 two more Zombies members had left school. Colin Blunstone started working as an insurance broker in London, while Rod Argent recalled, "After I'd taken my 'A' levels I deliberately didn't apply to university until it was too late to be accepted that year, because I desperately wanted something to happen with the band so that we could turn professional." Instead Argent was employed as a wages clerk at the Ballito's Hosiery Mill where the group would occasionally play the Saturday dance.

During 1963, as The Zombies were slowly graduating to bigger and bigger venues, occasionally visiting neighbouring towns, their repertoire started to change. The Shadows instrumentals, which were staple diet of the majority of British bands in the early sixties, had to go as more and more covers of American R&B artists found their way into the band's repertoire.

"Strange as it may seem, we always felt that we were rooted in R&B because of the kinds of things we were playing," Paul Atkinson recalled. "We were doing cover versions of R&B songs. What we ended up recording was completely different, but what we did on stage was very much rooted in R&B. We loved it, it was terrific. It's just that it wasn't quite the kind of music that Chris and Rod ended up writing."

While some US soul and rhythm 'n' blues records were starting to appear in UK shops, other records were less easy to find. "All the Motown stuff was easily available," Atkinson continued. "Even the early stuff was very popular. Increasingly, in London you could find some obscure American R&B records. Not so much in St Albans, but there was a store there called Green's. That was the record store in St Albans. We were regulars in there, and the guy who used to own it got obscure records in there because he knew we would buy them."

While The Zombies to all accounts were a fine rhythm 'n' blues band on stage, some radical changes would have to happen in order to turn them from a locally successful combo into a major international recording name. Quite simply, they would have to start writing their own material. By early 1963 such a thing was still virtually unheard of in Britain (the first Beatles records had only just started to come out), and really there wasn't much inspiration to draw on from America in this respect either – with one all-important exception.

Fronted by a slim, bespectacled young man from Lubbock, Texas, Buddy Holly's band The Crickets had made an immense impact on English teenage audiences even before their famous British tour of 1958. By adding what was then considered a hard, driving rock 'n' roll beat to his own simple, immensely beautiful melodies Holly had managed to create an artistically teasing cocktail, the effects of which would linger all the way through the Beat Boom, the 1970s glam and punk, and even into today's music. Not bad for someone who died at the age of 21 with only eighteen months of a recording career behind him.

Holly's popularity in Britain wasn't quite matched by his status at home. There was something about him that spoke to the Brits in particular. Apart from his music having an equivalent in the appealing simplicity of traditional British folk songs, it probably was important as well that he wasn't particularly foreign-looking from a British point of view; he didn't even have Presley's dangerous, Cherokee glint in the eye. Buddy Holly could, in fact, have been working in any chip-shop up and down Great Britain without anyone looking twice.

Two key members of The Zombies express immense admiration for The Crickets, namely Chris White and Colin Blunstone. John Lennon and Paul McCartney in Liverpool were devoted fans too. That was mainly what got them into writing songs themselves – they wanted to be like Buddy.

When they finally managed to get it right, the world would never be the same again.

6

The Beatles and the new Beatles

I n the very early sixties the music was getting a bit tired,"
Chris White opined. "It wasn't until The Beatles came
along that things changed, because up until that point
English music was copying or doing cover versions of American things, and the only homegrown product, I suppose,
was Cliff Richard and Johnny Kidd."

However, The Zombies weren't immediately taken over
by up-and-coming Beatlemania. Colin Blunstone recalls
not being particularly impressed by the Liverpool four's
first George Martin-produced single, "Love Me Do". Chris
White missed out on it altogether.

"The thing that really struck me was 'Please Please Me',"
he said. "I thought that was astounding. It had that thing
which Rod and I tried to use a lot, the clashing harmonies
and so on."

Blunstone joined in as a fan by the time of The Beatles'

first LP in 1963: "I thought they were staggering. I thought they were fantastic. I couldn't have been more of a fan of the Beatles than I was."

Likewise, Rod Argent stated, "At this time they were still writing stuff like 'P.S. I Love You', which is great. I love those early Beatles songs. I just love that innocence and naive quality on their very early things. It was so full of youthful energy and was such an explosion of happiness. Not saying that everything has to be like that, but it's a period that I do like to listen to. As soon as The Beatles came on the scene it had a major effect. We were already going at that time, and I desperately wanted to be in a band long before The Beatles came to the fore, but they opened so many doors for everybody."

As already mentioned, there were hardly any British groups writing and performing their own songs before The Beatles started this new trend. But that wasn't the only area in which they were inspiring to other young bands. As singers, arrangers and instrumentalists they made an equally important impression. Hugh Grundy:

"You listen to some of those early Beatles songs, and Ringo was very clever with his little patterns. I think that influenced me quite a bit. It also helped that Rod was keen on that sort of thing as well. He'd suggest things and between the two of us we'd work out something. That's how we came up with the pattern for 'She's Not There', which of course is a classic pattern these days."

At the same time, certain US artists still remained favourites with The Zombies members as well. Chris White highly praises The Everly Brothers, "the most underrated influence on modern music."

"From America I thought The Beach Boys were incredible," said Colin Blunstone. "But the artist I had most records of was Nina Simone. I think I had five or six albums of hers.

The first one I bought was *Nina Simone at the Town Hall*, and I used to play it all the time, particularly a track called 'Wild As The Wind'. I didn't try to sing along with her, I just found her records so atmospheric and moving. Furthermore, we'd all gone to see the Stones play when they'd just recorded 'Come On'. They were playing in a little club called Studio 51 just off Leicester Square. They completely blew us away. They were playing a lot of Chuck Berry and Bo Diddley. They were absolutely fantastic, and I also really loved their first album."

One thing that separated The Zombies from most other beat groups at the time was that they included a keyboard in their line-up. Previously, Rod Argent had found himself forced to make do with any old upright piano that came his way, stick some kind of microphone inside it and hope for a bit of amplification. To put it in another way, he hadn't really been audible apart from when he did the obligatory Jerry Lee Lewis runs up and down the keys. Now, working as a clerk at the Ballito's factory, he had managed to scrape enough money together to buy an electric piano, a Hohner Pianette Mk I.

The Pianette immediately became the group's main instrumental voice, since Paul Atkinson was mainly a rhythm guitarist who could throw in the occasional riff or solo. In fact, it wouldn't be far wrong to describe The Zombies as a guitar combo with the lead guitar substituted by a keyboard instrument. That was what gave them their unique sound, but possibly also what distanced them from some audiences in an era dominated by guitar groups.

Rod Argent became the master of the Hohner Pianette. In fact, he is probably the only person ever to make any sense of this peculiar little instrument. In his hands the otherwise very limited Pianette somehow came to life and to a large extent led the group through the main part of their three years with Decca Records. The instrument therefore seems worth spending a few words on.

"To play the Hohner Pianette you had to approach it in a slightly jazz sort-of-way," Rod Argent divulged to me. "It had a real bite to it. It was a brilliant sound. When I was in Argent I still used it. I loved it. They only made that particular model for a while, and then it became Mark II. The Mark I was the first electronic keyboard and it was just a revelation. Suddenly, there was this thing where you could actually hear what I was playing. It was wonderful."

Les Lambert, who had to struggle with keeping that very same Pianette alive some ten years later, recalled it less fondly:

"It's kind of akin to the Wurlizer electric pianos, but it's got no attack. They're both using metal reeds with little electric pick-ups, but in the Wurlizer the reeds are struck by a little hammer, sort of like a real piano. In the Pianette there's a piece of double-sided sticky tape at the end of each key, and when they are at rest the tape has a chance to stick to the reeds. Then when you strike the key it lifts the reed until the tape lets go of it and the reed goes back and says 'pling'. If you try and play it fast the tape doesn't have a chance to stick, and when the temperature changes the stickiness changes too, so under stage light they're useless. If you ever leave it in a dusty environment and something falls on to one of the keys and leaves it down so that the tape doesn't touch, then it's that note gone. The sticky tape gets dust on it and that's it, it's finished. You can put another piece of tape on, but it's special stuff and they don't sound the same if you try to do it with any other kind of tape. It's a nightmare! And of course like all Hohner stuff it's built like a German radiogram from the 1940s. They're terribly made."

At this point, and in fact a short while into the band's professional career, Chris White still played a home-made bass, while Hugh Grundy steadily added more bits to his drum kit.

Paul Atkinson had an acoustic steel-strung Zenith guitar: "My mother had bought that for me for £15 in 1961 from the local music store. It wasn't expensive, but it was a pretty well-made guitar. I added a couple of pick-ups to it and electrified it myself."

As the so-called Beat Boom swept Britain during 1963-64, groups like The Zombies suddenly achieved attention and opportunities to a degree they had probably never dared to dream of. Still, there was always the problem of how to break out of the local scene and make a larger impact. One possibility was to enter one of the many beat group competitions at the time. At this point the world hadn't acknowledged the fact that The Beatles were a unique phenomenon and everywhere the call was out to find other groups of a similar quality. These events, though often officially confined to the county in which they took place, sometimes gathered an audience of several thousand, mainly teenagers.

In the spring of 1964 the amusingly-named Herts Beat Competition ("Herts" is pronounced "hearts" and short for Hertfordshire), arranged by Watford Borough Council sponsored by *The Evening Standard*, proved to be just the springboard The Zombies needed. Paul Atkinson:

"Everyone around St Albans and Hatfield told us, 'You guys are bloody good. You're the best band around.' And frankly, we used to see the other bands and they were all pretty lame. Not being arrogant, it's true. The competition we just did for a laugh."

The Zombies entered the competition in the fifth heat, which was held at Watford Town Hall on 5 April 1964. Nine bands were competing that night, starting with Eddie Falcon and the Fournotes. The only participant of even the faintest renown (except, of course, from our heroes), Eddie

Falcon had released two singles in 1960 and 1961 on Columbia Records. However, it was the local Watford group D. and the Vostocks who appeared to be favourites until The Zombies, last on the bill, took the stage.

Starting with The Beatles' "You Can't Do That", the group then carried on with some R&B standards, including Muddy Waters' "I've Got My Mojo Working", sung by Rod Argent who also swapped his Hohner for the infamous mouth organ. However – according to a report in the *Watford And West Herts Post* – "the one which probably gave them the decision over all the rest was their own arrangement of 'Summertime'." Hugh Grundy:

"We'd never played as big a hall as that. We did our best. We played 'Summertime', which was totally different to anybody else. I think we dressed a little bit differently. Of course when we won that, to our amazement, we looked forward to the final."

The crowd was ecstatic as head of the judges, singer Sandra Barry, jumped on stage and enticed the group to perform as an encore with her The Shirelles' hit, "Boys". At this point The Zombies had been announced as winners, a decision no one could argue with. As drummer Garry Nicholls, member of the group that came second that night recalls:

"The Zombies quite frankly were a knock-out. It was nice to be there and see them at such an early stage. They were superb. They were head and shoulders above us, doing some really great R&B stuff. Far more my cup of tea than the stuff we were doing."

Chris White recalls, "I think everybody began to think then, 'Maybe something's started to happen here!'"

With a place in the competition final, Rod Argent was thinking that perhaps it would win the group a few points if they could perform one or two self-composed songs for the occasion. He had, in fact, written his first song several years earlier for The Bluetones (who recorded it on an acetate). According to Argent himself this song had "a million chords" and, like the material Chris White had been writing up until now, wasn't suitable for The Zombies' repertoire.

However, Argent now wrote specifically for his own group a new song titled "Hole In My Bucket" (soon to be retitled "It's Alright With Me"). It was a fairly standard rhythm 'n' blues tune in the Ray Charles mould, albeit with a surprising shift in tempo and feel during the jazzy bridge between second and third verse. The lyric seemingly combined two predominant themes in traditional blues as the singer partly warns his girlfriend that he has no assets to his name, partly that he will be forced to turn her down if she doesn't stay faithful to him. However, should she still choose to stay with him – and even love him – he will have no quibbles about it!

"It's Alright With Me" marks a remarkable beginning to a career that would eventually rank Rod Argent as one of the finest British songwriters of the period. Considering the youth and inexperience of the writer, certain features here are quite advanced, such as the way that the main chord sequence is imitated between each stanza in the form of a guitar riff. Equally interesting is the bridge where a Bb chord is dissolved into a G – a slightly unusual harmonic shift of a kind that can be found in many other Zombies songs throughout their career.

The very first studio session the group recorded comprised "Hole In My Bucket" and George Gershwin's famous "Summertime", the opening song from his 1935 "folk opera" *Porgy and Bess*. With less than two weeks to go before the competition final, the band laid down demo versions of these two numbers on 29 April 1964 at a studio called Jackson's in Rickmansworth.

"It was a very small, minor studio run by two brothers,"

Chris White explained. "Their father used to be the disc jockey, Jack Jackson. He used to be on Radio Luxembourg for Decca, and they now dealt in studio parts and things like that. That was the first studio we went to, and it was smaller than your normal bedroom. Very primitive two-track equipment."

Both tracks recorded on that day were very close in arrangement and performance to the versions released later, the main difference being a longer piano solo in the middle of "Summertime". Though this wasn't an original composition, the group had given it an arrangement that completely changed the shape of the song to the extent that it almost became their own. Most notably, the slow, flowing feel of the original arrangement is changed into a strict waltz-like tempo.

Chris White: "In an acoustic trio I used to play with, we were just a bass guitar and two guitarists. One of them was Michael Chaplin – we called him Chas – and he used to play 'Summertime' in 6/8, or whatever. So I suggested we'd do the same thing when I joined The Zombies. But then Rod also liked the version by Miles Davis, and it began to take its own shape. Those two influences were its starting points. The bass line I had probably made up already when I was with this other group."

The early demo version of "Summertime" finally appeared on the 1997 4-CD box set *Zombie Heaven*, released by Big Beat, where for some reason "Hole In My Bucket" aka "It's Alright With Me" is left out (cassette copies have for years been circulating among collectors). They were both cut only as acetates at the time.

The group was now concentrating their energy on the Herts Beat Competition final, which was to be held on 10 May at Watford Town Hall. Once more the panel of judges was led by singer Sandra Barry (who most famously recorded a single for Decca that same year backed by The Boys, who later turned into the superb George Martin-produced Mod group, The Action. She also recorded under several other names, such as Sandra Alfred and Sandra Browne. In the 1970s she reputedly returned to rock's underworld as Alice Springs of the band Slack Alice). Even more famous was the rest of the panel, consisting of none other than Shane Fenton (later Alvin Stardust) and his group The Fentones. (Fenton, a singer somewhere in the musical landscape between Adam Faith and Chris Farlowe, released nine singles for Parlophone between 1961 and 1964, enjoying minor hits with "I'm A Moody Guy" and "Cindy's Birthday".) The competition once again consisted of a long line of now-long forgotten local groups, The Zombies rounding off the show.

"You drew a card to see who would sing last," Colin Blunstone said. "It was obviously best to sing last. In the heat we were last, and in the final we were last. I think that was quite lucky."

Watford Town Hall held more than 1,200 people, so it was huge event for everyone involved. The hall was completely packed with people, since all the participating groups had brought their crowds of local followers to support them. "It was a bit like a football cup game," said Chris White. "Everybody was shouting and there were lots of banners, scarfs and bells."

In addition to this Hugh Grundy told me, "The stage was so big that each band could set up in one particular area. In those days you didn't have a great deal of equipment – an AC30 [a famous guitar amplifier with built-in loudspeakers], a foundation bass and a small PA. That was all you needed. You had to pick the straw for the position on the stage, and we picked the same position we had in the heat. We thought that was a good sign. All the bands were good and it was a fantastic evening. We had two or three coach-loads of fans who came across. They did make a noise for us. Those fans had only been acquired over months of playing in the smaller places, the dance halls and the places around St Albans and Hatfield. So when we asked them they pulled out for us. They all went on the coaches and came across and cheered us on. I'm sure that made all the difference."

On this occasion, The Zombies played a set of some nine or ten songs, including Argent's own "It's Alright With Me" (now bearing this title), "Summertime", Bob Bain's "I'm Going Home" (taken from a version by Gene Vincent) and "Got My Mojo Working".

In the *Watford And West Herts Post* the following day, journalist Peter Jackson reported:

When it was announced... that The Zombies had won, a solid wave of screams started from somewhere in the heights of the building and rolled around the room.

The Zombies themselves literally jumped for joy when they heard the results. Their pride at taking the first prize of £250 overflowed – but they wanted to make special mentions of their army of fans who made the short trek from Hertfordshire's "Beat City" and thank them for their vociferous support.

It may come as a surprise to older readers, but without a word of a lie, I saw and heard mothers screaming their heads off when they won.

"My parents came along," recalled Paul Atkinson. "It was a big, a huge success. It was terrific. We had the biggest audience we'd ever played to and we won the first prize and a recording deal! We also met this guy from Decca Records, Dick Rowe, whom we later found out was *the* Dick Rowe, Head of A&R. Some of the other guys don't remember this, but I have a very clear memory of sitting backstage at Watford Town Hall after we'd won and sort of basking in the glow, coming off this high, and a guy comes in wearing a dark three-piece suit and a tie, white shirt, very business-

The Zombies

like. To us he was an older guy; he must have been all of 35! He says, 'Ahoy, boys! My name's Dick Rowe from Decca Records.' He whoops a piece of paper out of his pocket and says, 'Here's a recording contract. We'd be happy to offer it to you on behalf of Decca Records. You guys are great. I know you're all under-age, so take this home, show your parents and give me a call.' He turned around and we never saw him again. He never came to recording sessions. Maybe Rod or the others met him, but I never saw him again. We didn't find it strange at the time because we didn't know any different. But looking back on it, it sounded very strange."

I asked Grundy if he, like Paul Atkinson, recalled the Decca representative approaching the group after their victory. "Yeah," he replied. "I remember him, absolutely. 'Sign this, sign that, I'll make you big stars,' and all the rest of it."

Dick Rowe failed in making the evening's winner sign the contract he had handed them. Instead, it seems that he did manage to strike a deal with the number two group, called The Beat Six, from Hemel Hempstead (a group of that name released a solitary single for Decca later in the year).

Typically, The Zombies didn't allow themselves to get so overwhelmed that they lost their better judgement. Instead, as their parents would have suggested, they took their time and surveyed their options before signing their names to anything.

7

Go for it!

Winning £250 (quite a substantial sum of money in 1964), and on top of that a recording deal, was very much the kind of break-through Rod Argent had been hoping for during the "dullest year of his life" as a clerk at Ballito's. There was now a realistic possibility for his group to go professional:

"I said to my parents, 'That's what I'm gonna do.' I had got a place at university, I was accepted at Hull, so they sat me down and said, 'Think about it. Are you sure that this is really what you want to do?' When I said, 'Yes, it is without question,' they supported me 100 percent. They were always great like that."

Chris White was in a similar position. He was getting towards the end of his training to become an art teacher. In fact, had just signed up for his final year when the debate about whether to go professional or not came up. "My father said, 'Go for it. You can always do teaching.' He was always encouraging and he supported the band, because he enjoyed music."

Hugh Grundy: "We all had a sort of fall-back. All the guys had done their schooling, they had university places, I had a career at the bank, so there was always that fall-back. We knew we could always go back to it if we wanted to, and this opportunity would never ever come again. So best we take it, grab it by the balls and have a go for it right now! Our parents were understanding, probably a little bit against it, but all of one mind thinking, 'If that's what the boys want to do we'll let them do it, because you never know what it can lead to.'"

Colin Blunstone had expected his mother and father to be sceptical about this new dubious career move, yet he was in for a surprise. "They obviously thought it was best that I just got this rock 'n' roll thing out of my system. Up until recently [1999] they were still waiting for me to get a real job! I supposed that all the parents accepted what we were doing, except one pair who weren't very keen. The other four sets of parents were really quite open to the idea of what we were doing, and quite supportive. They thought it was a good thing for young people to go out and have a go. I was amazed at my parents' reaction, absolutely amazed. What they'd seen was that lately we really did have quite a following and they could see that something was happening. I think that probably helped."

The one pair of parents Blunstone mentions as being less willing to let their protégé into professional rock 'n' roll were that of Paul Atkinson. As the junior of the group he was still at school and had his "A" level exams coming up by the summer of 1964. Plans were for him go to university in September to study Anthropology and Modern Languages.

"My parents said, 'Forget about it. We prefer that you get

your 'A' levels. If you get three 'A' levels you can do whatever you like.' So I worked like hell and studied a lot and made sure I got my 'A' levels, otherwise I was gonna be screwed. I didn't want the band to leave me behind, which was what they would have to do. They'd made plans to get another guitar player; I think it was Rod talking to Jim Rodford, and I think Jim was prepared to switch from bass to guitar to join The Zombies. That would have been perfectly reasonable if I couldn't carry on.

"I did get three 'A' levels, thank God, in English, French and German. I really studied very hard. I burned the midnight oil many times, because I was absolutely terrified of failing. I remember staying up on black coffee the night before one of the exams, and I'm sure that the minute it was over I forgot everything. But I did pass, that was the important thing. I got my university place confirmed and then my parents relented and said, 'Well, it's up to you.' My mother wasn't very happy about it, but we did turn professional in July."

Colin Blunstone: "One of our problems was that we had to serve our apprenticeship in the public eye. We were a school band playing at little local dances up until the very day before we became professional. And four weeks later we had a hit record. We didn't have a hit record first and *then* became professional.

"We decided we were gonna have a go, all of us. We bought ourselves a van, and we decided we were going to be professional musicians. We didn't know for how long. You have to accept that if you're lucky enough to get success, of course you accept it graciously when and where it comes. But if we could have chosen, it would have been better to have come a year or so later when we could have made some of our mistakes in a more private environment. We needed to get out on the road and knock a few edges off and toughen up a bit, really."

Following their victorious night at Watford Town Hall, The Zombies had several other offers apart from Decca's. It was felt that they needed outside advice to pick and choose, and thus the hunt was on for some kind of management and publishing deal.

The first manager the group approached was called George Cooper. "He had a bit of a reputation of being tough," recalled Colin Blunstone. "We went to this very American-type house, like a deluxe bungalow. We sat down right at the edge of the seats. He said, 'Would you like a drink, boys?' And he brought over whiskies and gins and everything. We were all frightened he was going to drug us! So we wouldn't have a drink. It was a very stiff and unsuccessful meeting.

"Then we met this other guy who was even funnier. We all went to his flat and the discussion went on. He had a dress-ing gown on. I don't remember what he had underneath – I don't think he had trousers on. We had a chat and it wasn't really going anywhere. He belonged to another era, a differ-ent generation to us. He came to the door to see us off – and he locked himself out! So there he was stuck in this block of flats with just a dressing gown on, and we had to get around to the back of the block of flats. There was a very small lift the size to put a dustbin in. That's how they got the dustbins up and down. He had to crouch down in this and we had to hoist him back up to his flat. I swear to you I wasn't looking up to see if he was wearing anything. I really didn't want to know. After such an inglorious start I think it would have been a little foolhardy to further that relationship."

After these episodes it dawned on the band that getting a decent deal in British show-business was not as easy as they had imagined. In fact, they now had to seek advice in order to choose between the people who were offering them advice! Luckily, with The Zombies there was always a cousin or an uncle you could lean on. Chris White:

"The Zombies never received any writing or recording advances at all, but we did sign good contracts because our music publishers were also our producers. They were Ken Jones and Joe Roncoroni, both of whom are dead now. I was introduced to them because we were offered some contracts after winning the competition, and my dad said, 'Go see my uncle Ted.' He was the one who had been a conscientious objector during the Second World War and got in a prisoner of war camp, and he suggested for us to go and see his friend Ken Jones. We had these different contracts, and Ken said, 'That's a good clause in that contract... no I wouldn't do that, I wouldn't.' I said, 'Well, what can *you* offer us?' He said, 'Well, I didn't know you were coming for that, but I'll offer you the best of all of them.' Which meant that after 10,000 sales we had our own publishing company and we still to this day get 85% of both the royalties as artists and, well, 50% of the songwriting, because that was the standard thing."

All the band members were very happy with Ken Jones, who would become their producer throughout their time with Decca. Jones was renowned in his day as a band leader, an arranger, and a writer of incidental TV music. Through their company Marquis Enterprises he and his partner, Joe Roncoroni, also owned the publishing on some successful American records that had been issued in Britain. The arrangement they struck up with The Zombies meant that the group would be recording with them on an independent basis, and then the master tapes would be leased to a record label.

"Fortunately, and unlike what happened to many other groups, Ken and Joe were totally honest," Paul Atkinson said. "When you think of the odds of that happening it's quite amazing. They were gents."

Today, The Zombies are still known as one of the few '60s UK beat groups to have made any money on their endeavours. Show-business at that time wasn't exactly over-crowded with honest and warmhearted promoters doing their utmost to make their clients rich. With the majority of bands coming from working-class environments and being without any experience in business, many lives were quite literally signed away during those years. Probably, it was The Zombies' social background that saved them from this particular kind of disaster.

"We weren't looking for a ticket out," recalls Paul Atkinson. "This wasn't our *one* chance, whereas a lot of bands in England at that time viewed recording contracts as their way out of the coal mine, or the factory, or whatever. That certainly wasn't the situation with any of us. We all, individually, could have gone on to university and done well."

8

Well, let me tell you...

Before entering the studio to record their first single The Zombies presented Ken Jones with the acetates from their previous session. Not surprisingly, he was particularly impressed with "Summertime".

"We'd played that for a long time," Blunstone explained. "Two or three years, so we knew it backwards. I think that was one of the best tracks we ever did."

Ken Jones also came to see the band play at St Albans Market Hall on 29 April (they day after they had performed a gig with Billy J Kramer in Watford, yet another bonus included in winning the Herts Beat Competition). Ken Jones had previously encouraged Rod Argent to write some more of his own material, and after the performance Argent told him that he had been working on a new song which had the working title "No One Told Me". The two of them sat down at a piano and Argent played the song for the producer. At this point it only had one verse and Ken Jones, suitably impressed, suggested adding one extra verse to it and rehearsing it for the up-and-coming recording session.

I asked Rod Argent how he had come to write the song in the first place.

"I was at home," he said. "I was living at home and I wrote it very much for the band, very much with Colin in mind. I wrote it for the session basically. I wrote it for Colin's range, and I could hear him singing it in my mind. For a start, I was listening to all my old blues records. There was a John Lee Hooker song called 'No One Told Me', which doesn't sound anything like 'She's Not There', but it has 'no one told me' as its first line. That just suggested the metre of the first line. The chord sequence, which started off as just being Am to D, was used in two or three songs that I liked. There was a Betty Carter song, and there was also an old Brian Hyland song which used that chord sequence. That all appealed to me, and really that's where that opening chord sequence came from. Then the metre of the lyric suggested the melody to me. After that I just had it in my head to build it to a climax.

"It's really quite an unusually constructed song, when you look at it. It's in three little sections. It was in my mind to build up the excitement, and I wanted to use the metre of the actual lyrics to propel it towards that final note. So the idea was of having the final section just on one note with chords changing underneath it, but with displaced rhythms. The accentuation of the words 'way', 'acted', and 'colour', those are displaced accents in the metre. That was almost a poetic urge I had, to move it along that metre."

One of the most noteworthy features, not only in "She's Not There" but in The Zombies' catalogue of songs as a whole, is the way chords are sometimes allowed to shift between major and minor (*see under "Chords" in Glossary*).

"I'd heard that somewhere and really liked the effect of the D major going to the D minor, with the bass playing the *thirds*. I suppose that was quite unusual at the time, because most people just played the root notes. I really wrote the song with that incredible arrogance and naivety you only have when you're eighteen years old. I thought, 'I can write something that's as good as The Beatles and it'll come out and be No. 1.' And it did! While I was completely excited and knocked out, it wasn't unexpected to me. I just thought, 'This is what happens.' Of course, I came down to earth with a bump very quickly when something didn't happen. All in all, I think the freshness of it, the fact that we were so young and naive when we went in to do it, contributed. I think it still sounds fresh today."

Incidentally, there is one more change between minor and major in the song, namely the very last chord in each chorus where an A minor chord is lifted up to an A major.

"I can remember rehearsing 'She's Not There'," Colin Blunstone said. "It was the second song Rod ever played to me that he'd written. In those days we used to rehearse one song all day. Just play it, and play it, and play it. I think there's a lot to be said for that. You get it so ingrained in your being that nobody can ever go wrong on this song and you can perform it in a different way compared to if you're not quite sure of it. I remember thinking, 'This could really do something.'"

Chris White recalled Rod Argent presenting "She's Not There" to him around the piano at Argent's mother's house.

"It was absolutely fascinating," White said. "The song was breathtaking in its approach. We worked on some ideas and found out what to play in the bass. We tried all sorts of different things. That was Rod's first real experience of songwriting."

In the lyric Argent wrote for the song, the narrator complains about his girlfriend having left him. She has obviously led him on and made false promises. The narrator's main criticism, however, is not aimed at the girl, but at his friends who knew what kind of girl she was and failed to warn him.

This is an unusual feature which can be found repeatedly in early Zombies songs, where the narrator is addressing not the girl he is in love with, nor the world in general, but a friend of his, another boy. In a sense, what we hear is one part only of a two-way conversation. The Beatles used – perhaps even invented – the same technique with "She Loves You", something Paul McCartney has spoken proudly of in interviews. While innovative, the idea also has a juvenile feel to it – the notion that you approach a person you are in love with through a third person rather than face-to-face is equivalent to the notes circulating in the classrooms of any secondary school.

In the case of "She's Not There" there is a similarly strong feeling of adolescence. However, the circumstances are different as the narrator is directly involved in the drama; in The Beatles' case the narrator is but a messenger (and the news is good, another significant difference of course). Furthermore, "She's Not There" has an aura of taking place in a kind of boys-only world, where girls are something so strange, mysterious and beyond all understanding that you can't even blame them for anything. Instead, you blame your friend for not having warned you about certain, particularly dangerous examples of the species.

Since this feeling of inability to communicate properly with the opposite sex is exceedingly common in early songs by both Rod Argent and Chris White, it obviously raises the question whether or not the all-boy environment they had been part of at school was responsible.

"I had a sister who was eleven years older than me and lived away from home," Chris White told me, "I didn't really know her, so to all intents and purposes I was an only child. Rod had a baby sister, but he's always in a world of his own anyway. Paul Atkinson had a brother, Hugh Grundy was an only child. Colin Blunstone was an only child. So we didn't have much feminine influence. I don't think we had any failure to communicate with the opposite sex – far from it from about fifteen – but treating them as another human being, maybe so."

On the same issue, Rod Argent said, "The thing was, we all went to parties and we all mixed with girls and we all took girls out and we all chased girls and all that was going on and it was great. From the time we were in The Zombies we were lucky because there were girls around who wanted to know us just because we had some sort of identity. At the same time we did all to go all-boys schools, and the fact was that we weren't around girls all the time. You had to manufacture situations to actually meet girls."

Such statements are only vaguely supportive of my analysis, but then I have to say that I generally found both White and Argent quite reluctant to connect their song lyrics with any real life experiences at all, claiming more-or-less that all their writings were attempts either to produce something that would match the melancholy of Colin Blunstone's voice (Chris White's argument), or simply a matter of putting down something that was *comme il faut* for all other songwriters at the time (Rod Argent). This, however, was strongly contradicted by other group members who, like myself, seem to feel that profound and personal experiences must have been involved in order to achieve anything so artistically strong. "Rod wouldn't have told you all the finer details," Hugh Grundy said, "but... his songs were obviously based around relationships – the successes and the failures and his views on life and relationships as he grew up. I know his songs are all about that. Of course they were."

The other two members, Blunstone and Atkinson, both hold similar views with regard to Chris White. However, without more participation from the writers themselves an approach from this angle is impossible and probably also disrespectful. Moreover, I doubt that the issue is all that important. The writers have handed their songs over to the world, leaving it up to us to choose what we want to do with them; the really interesting aspect isn't what motivated them to write in the first place, but the effect that the songs can have on us, their listeners.

Personally, I have no problem with recognising the emotional universe in "She's Not There". I've had stranded relationships after which my only comfort was to imagine my former partner about as deceased-looking as the one Rod Argent describes in his song (using past tenses only!) I can identify with the naked helplessness in Colin Blunstone's voice, and his near-hysterical hitting the high notes during the chorus as he recalls the looks of his former partner. For me, these experiences go back many years, but that doesn't mean a song like "She's Not There" can't be relevant to me now that I am in my forties. At least they can serve as a sound reminder that I don't need any "second youth", because it really wasn't particularly glorious or wonderful the first time around.

9

Let there be drums

T he Zombies entered Decca's West Hampstead Studio No. 2 on 12 June 1964 to record four songs – "It's Alright With Me", "She's Not There", "You Make Me Feel Good" and "Summertime".

"The place is now the headquarters of the English Opera," Paul Atkinson told me, "but it was known as Decca Recording Studios at the time. We all went together. We drove there together and we went in together. We were all very excited. We started recording about 1 or 2 in the afternoon and we recorded the songs very quickly."

If anyone expected the group to be shivering with nerves, they didn't know these guys.

Rod Argent: "Nowadays I know just how much can go wrong, but back then we didn't see any of that, we just thought, 'Yeah, we're great. We can go into the recording studio and the song will sound great.' The only records we'd seen being made were by Elvis in some of his films, which isn't quite realistic."

Chris White also recalled having Presley films as his main reference point for what was about to happen, his first impression being surprise at how young the engineers were at the studio. "In fact, during our first recording session the engineer had been to a wedding, and he was pissed for the rest of the session. Gus Dudgeon was tape operator, and then he took over. It was his first session ever. He engineered all we did down at Decca."

Colin Blunstone: "The engineer was called Teddy [Johnson]; I thought he'd been to a wedding, but I've heard other people say that he'd just been out for lunch. He was very drunk and very aggressive. He was actually carried out halfway through the session with one bloke on each arm and one bloke on each leg. We met him again as he worked on tracks with us after that, and he was a delightful character. But on that session he was very aggressive. In 'You Make Me Feel Good' there are little bits where Rod goes, 'Ah-ha.' This guy said, 'If you're gonna bloody ah-ha, I'm gonna bloody...' In fact, he didn't say 'bloody', he said something else. And this is coming down the can, very loud, and we were getting a bit nervous. I remember I thought, 'Well, if this is recording, I don't think it's for me.' Anyway, he was carried out and his assistant took over."

The backing track for the second song to be recorded on that day, "She's Not There", took seven attempts to get right.

It is amazing to discover what hides underneath the surface of this song. Analysing it, you suddenly discover the versatile influences Argent has mentioned coming together, from simple blues through modern jazz to the open-voice approach of church singing. Perhaps the most amazing thing is the ease and instinctive approach with which it is carried out, and the fact that all these seemingly incongruous influences are melted into the format of a straightforward two-minute Beat Boom single.

The arrangement is striking right from the first note, the bass being the main driving ingredient, with drums and electric piano playing individual patterns. The guitar doesn't come in until the bridge in each verse, and the backing vocals drift in and out, singing harmonies below the lead voice.

The song has a dynamic build-up split into three sections, starting in a low, subdued mode, moving into the mid-tempo stride of the bridge, after which all members are hammering it out eight-to-the-bar building up to the chorus with the voice almost hysterically clinging to the same high note. Then it stops and starts all over again.

The second verse follows the pattern of the first; however before the third verse, instead of stopping and winding down, the band returns in high-impact mode, the drums playing a standard 4/4 rhythm (with inserted tom-tom beats) and the vocal replaced by a flowing, jazz-inspired electric piano solo until the bridge, where the voices come back in.

Everything about the performance on this record is perfect, though it can't be denied that the most overwhelming element is the lead singing. Completely different from anything known in the rock world before or since, Colin Blunstone swings effortlessly between his normal range and falsetto, managing to send shivers down the listener's spine from the first stanza onward. The lyric may be pure teenage drama, but Blunstone reminds us that not only are such emotions brutally real for any young person experiencing them, they can also mark you for the rest of your life, however much you would prefer to laugh them off as pubescent embarrassment.

Like all other songs officially released by The Zombies at

the time, "She's Not There" was recorded on a four-track tape machine and then mixed into mono on another tape. According to Chris White, this was principally how the instruments and voices would be spread over the individual tracks:

Track 1: Bass, Drums, Guitar
Track 2: Piano
Track 3: Harmonies
Track 4: Lead vocal

Tracks 1, 2 and 4 would be recorded simultaneously (known as a "backing track"), though the voice laid down at this point was only a "guide vocal", which would later be wiped and re-recorded at the same time as the two harmonies (performed by Argent and White) were added.

When this part of the work was over, the band was sent away and the final mixing was left to the engineers and the producer. In the case of "She's Not There", this is the point where things became somewhat mysterious.

First, it must be explained that the kind of recording procedure described in the above was from start to finish aimed at making mono records only. However, during the late sixties and early seventies, record companies developed the idea that their customers preferred to hear all music in stereo even if it wasn't meant to be stereo in the first place. Hence they would sometimes take mono versions of songs and fool around with them in the studio, turning up the bass in one channel, adding more reverb in the other, and so on. This technique, known as "electronically enhanced stereo", should be avoided by all music lovers.

Another, much better (but still unsatisfactory) method was to dig out the old multi-track master tapes and re-mix them from scratch. This, however, caused two kinds of problem. First, the resultant mix would more often than not have a peculiar stereo separation, since instruments that were recorded on the same track obviously had to stay together in the stereo image of the new mix. As a result, the stereo mix that Decca made of "She's Not There" at a later stage had drums, bass and guitar on one side, piano on the other side, and lead vocal and harmonies in the middle. In comparison, a modern stereo mix would seek to get both bass and vocals in the middle, drums recorded in stereo but anchored around the middle, harmonies flowing all over the stereo image, with polyphonic instruments such as guitars and keyboards spread on either side.

The second problem with this kind of approach is that during the original mono mixing procedure, extra instruments or vocal harmonies were sometimes added. This was done by taking the music signal coming out of the four-track tape recorder and sending it through a mixing console, at the same time as an extra instrument or vocal – done live – was sent into the console via a fifth channel. It would all be mixed together simultaneously and put down on a separate tape. This tape presented the final mix that would go to the pressing plant for production.

To sum it up, digging out 1960s four-track master tapes for stereo mixes is a bad option, as it makes for unnatural stereo separation, and means that overdubs added in the mono mix-down aren't available. The solution? Stick with mono!

What the stereo mix of "She's Not There" mainly suffers from is the lack of certain features in the percussion department, when compared with the original mono single. The Zombies have never denied that an extra snare drum beat was added to the main drum pattern during the first part of each verse, though it isn't quite clear why this was necessary. Rod Argent told me that, "Hugh couldn't get it right." However, existing live recordings not long afterwards suggest that Grundy had no particular problems in this respect.

Tape operator/engineer Gus Dudgeon recalls differently in the notes for the 4-CD box set *Zombie Heaven*. He suggests that the seemingly small but crucial addition to the recording was probably made on the initiative of engineer Terry Johnson, who might even have played it himself as he was an accomplished drummer who had recently toured with P.J. Proby.

But the case doesn't end there. Playing the stereo and mono versions back to back you discover that not only is the added snare drum incredibly active all the way through – adding much more than the beats to the main riff – there are also extra cymbals and tom-toms heavily featured on the mono track. Furthermore the whole style of drumming and the drum kit itself sounds different from Hugh Grundy's original playing.

As none of the band members was present during the mix-down, all we have are Gus Dudgeon's somewhat vague recollections (it has not been possible to track down Terry Johnson for an interview and for obvious reasons his memories could well be somewhat blurred). However, putting the facts together there seems to be only one explanation for what occurred on 12 June 1964 after The Zombies had left Decca's West Hampstead studios.

In all probability, listening back to the recording in a more sober state, studio engineer Terry Johnson must have felt tremendously panicky. With the sessions being handed over to a junior tape operator, the drums had been worryingly poorly recorded on all tracks bar one, "It's Alright With Me", (which was put down by Johnson himself while he was still sober). Trying to toughen up the sound during the mix was out of the question, because the drums were on the same track as the guitar and the bass, meaning that attempts to change the drum sound radically would considerably change the sounds of these instruments as well, and not in a desirable manner.

Though it was Gus Dudgeon who had engineered the problematic tracks, Johnson was of course still responsible for the session, a session with the group who had just won the prestigious Herts Beat Competition. In fact, the recording was part of the winning prize. As a consequence, a lot of people – including a few keen journalists over at *The Evening Express* – were expecting to see some truly excellent results for their money. That was why Decca Studios had been hired, not exactly an unknown little business. If the news came out that one of their chief engineers had drunk himself senseless, been abrasive towards a group of recording artists, and eventually been carried out and sent home in a cab, there was a good chance his days with the company would be over.

I suggest that in the light of these circumstances Johnson decided something drastic had to be done. It had already been suggested that a drumbeat be added to the main rhythmic pattern of "She's Not There", but in fact Terry Johnson can be heard throughout the entire mix-down of the track. After that, he repeated this procedure with "Summertime" and "You Make Me Feel Good", albeit in a considerably more restrained frame of mind. (To add to the general feeling of desperation, this working-method was illegal at the time. In order to do overdubs you had to apply to the Musicians' Union first, a time consuming procedure which normally resulted in a negative reply. Obviously, Terry Johnson did not have time for anything like that.)

The ironic thing is that not only did Johnson thus salvage the recording of "She's Not There", he also furnished it with a unique, powerful sound that probably gave it a kick-start towards the top of the charts. It was truly a blessing in disguise! In fact, this very idea of using two drum kits – one a full kit, the other just consisting of a snare, two toms and a cymbal – is very close indeed to what Elvis Presley was using in the early '60s post-army period and part of the secret behind the powerful sound on albums such as *Elvis Is Back*.

If my assumptions here are correct, they raise two new questions. First, how on earth did Terry Johnson manage to sober up enough during the afternoon to play the drums? Second, does this new information diminish the reputation of the group and their first hit record?

With regard to the latter question, I don't think so. Nothing can change the fact that it was Hugh Grundy who played with the group when the track was recorded, and his drumming is well featured. He was then still a player in the making and progressed incredibly over the following months as the band's status rapidly grew, but it is nevertheless his original energy and unmistakable style that drives the song along. If the drumming on the stereo mix of "She's Not There" sounds a bit feeble, it is because of the way it was recorded. In fact, there are some fine details in Grundy's playing which are unfortunately drowned out by the overdubs on the mono mix.

The B-side of "She's Not There" was taken up by "You Make Me Feel Good", a song written by Chris White. It was originally based on a two-chord riff shifting between E major and G# minor with the vocal staying on the note b. However, Rod Argent suggested at some early stage that the second chord be dissolved into a G# major, meaning that the melody line had to change slightly as well (now shifting between b and b#). Though Argent and White weren't writing songs together as such, they would sometimes suggest such changes to each other's compositions.

Trying to reconstruct Chris White's original song as it was before the incorporation of the new change suggested by Rod Argent, I found that the first version has a distinct melancholic spirit to it which unfortunately has a tendency towards becoming monotonous. Furthermore, the new chord change makes the song slightly more harmonically adventurous. That the change was suggested by Rod Argent is ironic, since Chris White would subsequently prove the more unorthodox of the two writers.

At a brief glance "You Make Me Feel Good" appears to be a rare example of a happy and positive lyric from the early repertoire of The Zombies. That would go hand in hand with Argent's suggestion to substitute a minor chord with a major. However, the positive statement in the lyric falls apart on closer scrutiny. The narrator's declaration that he won't even attempt to put into words why he loves his girlfriend, simply because his feelings for her are so strong that such explanation isn't necessary, does not convince the listener.

It appears that what has prompted the exclamation in the first place is the girlfriend's demand for some form of reason why he loves her. It takes no expert on womanhood to see that she is either nervous that his feelings have cooled off, or she is simply fishing for a compliment. He, however – perhaps coming from the great British tradition of separating the sexes at secondary school level – replies in a subdued, irritated fashion and with stringent male logic that love is about feelings, not words. Why does she have to ask him this? Surely, he never asks himself such questions. She makes him feel good and, hence, he doesn't have to "justify" himself to her, as she "surely" ought to be aware at this point in their relationship.

Musically, the song is pure Beat Boom. With its midtempo performance and accentuation on the first beat and second off-beat of each bar it is also a blueprint for how a typical Zombies song would sound during most of their Decca period. The Beatles have often been mentioned as an inspiration for the track, yet you could also include other Liverpool groups at the time such as The Searchers or The Merseybeats. As mentioned, Grundy's drums are not recorded too well but at least it is revealing – and unusual for the time – to hear a loud bass drum working closely with the bass guitar. The overdubbed drums on the original mono mix only make up for the lack of power in the recording of the backing track by basically double-tracking Hugh Grundy's simple-but-efficient playing (hitting the snare drum with a double beat every other time makes for a nice "groovy" effect).

Otherwise, what wins you over is the overall sound made up by perfect ingredients. The Hohner Pianette has all the proclaimed bite and penetration, the delicately played acoustic guitar a full-bodied sound, almost like a 12-string, while the bass (keeping to the root notes) is strong and powerful. Above all, the lead vocal and the harmonies are stunningly beautiful. The song has a short, bluesy instrumental introduction and ends in a pure Beatles fashion, with a brief chord progression descending chromatically from G major back to E major.

It may be of interest that the backing track for the song was recorded slightly differently to normal procedure, as the later stereo mix suggests the guitar was put on to the same track as the electric piano.

Where "She's Not There" was strong in originality, "You Make Me Feel Good" sounds like an all-convincing 1964 Mersey Beat classic, making it difficult for the group and their producer to decide which should go on the A-side of the coming single. Even when the band members received test pressings of the record, it wasn't yet decided which song would literally come out on top. The eventual choice of "She's Not There" proved the right one, but in retrospect it might have been cleverer if the less convincing "It's Alright

With Me" (from the same day) had gone on the flip, leaving a strong composition in the vaults for the next single, while still having the amazing "Summertime" waiting in the wings as well. You could argue that Ken Jones wanted to make the debut single as much of a knock-out as possible and thus went for a strong flip-side, but in reality no one cared much for B-sides in those days and it probably wouldn't have made any difference to the success of "She's Not There". Colin Blunstone recalled his feelings at the time:

"Perhaps this has a lot to do with being eighteen, but I thought that all three of those songs could possibly be hits."

Naïve or not, he was probably right. Most members of the group still recall their very first session at Decca Studios as the best they ever recorded there.

What remains to be noted is that The Zombies debut single "She's Not There"/"You Make Me Feel Good" saw release a mere six weeks after it had been recorded, on 24 July 1964. Youthful self-assuredness guaranteed that no one would be in for a big surprise if it became a hit. Nevertheless, spending Christmas in New York that very same year was probably not even on the most far-seeing agenda.

10

The swots are coming

During August 1964, as "She's Not There" started climbing towards the Top 10 in the British charts, The Zombies found themselves extending their touring activities to the entire nation. They signed with Tito Burns, a major agent and promoter at the time, who sent them out on a gruelling string of one-nighters up and down the country. "Burns looked after a lot of American artists when they came over, Bob Dylan for instance," Colin Blunstone related to me. "He also managed The Searchers and Dusty Springfield. Because of that we worked with those people a lot, especially with The Searchers."

Inevitably, with their new status, The Zombies had to get themselves what is now known as a "roadie". "That was Paul Arnold's brother," Blunstone continued. "His name was Terry Arnold, and he had been our manager while we were amateurs. He used to help us get dates and things like that. Then when we signed to Tito Burns, Terry Arnold became sort of a tour manager."

Unfortunately, things weren't well between Terry Arnold and Colin Blunstone. In fact, the other members frequently feared that fights would break out between the two. On top of everything else, Arnold struggled with a bad back and thus couldn't carry any equipment. Hence, the band had to carry their own instruments and amplifiers. With all the gigs they were now getting, it meant long hours of driving and lots of hard work besides getting up on stage and playing. Paul Atkinson:

"We had a beat-up old Commer, a red and white van which had terribly leaky doors. It was freezing in the winter. We used to wrap ourselves in our sleeping bags. Terry drove it, and Hugh drove it sometimes, and Chris drove it sometimes. Rod and Colin and I never did."

In the midst of all this, Argent and White were trying to write new songs for more releases and on 13 August they entered Ryemuse Studios in South Molton Street, London, to lay down demo versions of three fresh, self-composed tracks, namely "Woman", "Kind Of Girl" and "Leave Me Be".

Listening to these recordings today (they became officially available in 1997 with the *Zombie Heaven* box set), you get a pretty good idea of the band's true sound at the time. Demos often sound weaker than final professional recordings, and this was under-rehearsed material – nevertheless there is no denying that The Zombies were still a group seriously in need of a producer's guidance. Their youthfulness and inexperience is striking, and when comparing these with the tracks laid down at Decca Studios some two weeks later, it becomes obvious how much Ken Jones at this stage contributed to the group's recording style.

The West Hampstead session took place on 31 August

and comprised the three earlier-recorded songs plus another new composition by Rod Argent, "Sometimes".

The song that would grace the A-side of the next single was Chris White's "Leave Me Be". On the whole, the track sounds entirely different to "She's Not There", yet a closer look reveals a number of striking similarities. For example, the choice of key, A minor, and the incorporation of both D minor and D major chords. Also, both have a dynamic build-up/fall-down arrangement with a three-part structure, a verse leading into an inner bridge leading into the chorus. The emphasis in both is on melodic quality.

Lyrically, the two songs also relate in the sense that they are both built on the notion of one guy complaining to another about his girlfriend. The narrator's sense of total hopelessness and his inability to break out of his predicament is a main feature in both cases.

It is characteristic of White's way of writing not to use particularly unusual chords, though in this case he does incorporate an F major 7th [see Glossary under "Major 7th chords"]. What he does instead is write unusual chord sequences; most notably, this song is in the key of A minor, yet the home chord of A minor does not occur until the very end of the song. That is highly unusual and in this case an essential feature, since it is the use of *tonic* (the chord corresponding to the key) that gives the listener a feeling of "coming home". By avoiding it on "Leave Me Be" White grabs hold of his listener and keeps him in a form of rootless suspense akin to the lyric's expression of despair, not allowing you the sense of rest until the very last note of the song.

Of course, songwriters don't think too much of such things when they write. They don't construct by reversed analysis – they use mainly their natural talent and what is in the back of their minds. In Chris White's case it almost appears to be

a matter of consciously wanting to stay theoretically unconscious:

"When I'm writing, something comes in my head and then
I have to find it on the instrument. I'm not musically liter-
ate. So what I do is I write what I hear in my head and
then try something else. But it's always in my head. It's like,
you know Michaelangelo used to say about sculpture that he
didn't carve marble, he set the figure free from the marble,
and that's what it always felt like for me, writing songs. I
could see this picture very hazily and was waiting for it to
come clear, musically speaking. So that's the way I write,
and without any knowledge of the rules of music. It's just
what I can hear. Sometimes I reach a point where I think,
'Where do I want to go in the melody here?' And sometimes
it's an unusual jump, and then I find a different root in the
bass and then play around a bit and then suddenly find the
exact move I want to make."

As a keyboardist and former choir singer, Rod Argent was
bound to be more theoretically conscious, yet his methods
of writing at this point weren't too dissimilar to White's.
Rod Argent:

"I met Pat Metheny before he became famous in America.
Someone introduced us, and I'd just seen him play and was
completely knocked out. He hadn't made his name and it
was just this tiny little theatre in America. I was amazed,
because Pat Metheny said, 'Rod Argent... "She's Not There"!'
He said, 'All that modal stuff, that was the record which
made me think I could pursue the direction I wanted to go
with fusion music.' I thought, 'What's modal about "She's
Not There"? It's only A minor to D.' So I went back and
listened to what I was playing, and I was actually playing
modally around those chords. I was actually playing a little
modal line, a scale. I thought, 'Blimey, it is!' And then I
thought, 'That's really only because I was listening to all the

Miles Davis stuff.' I hadn't thought, 'Okay, I'll do a modal thing now like Miles does.' It was just a sound that was running around my head because I'd listened to a lot of that stuff, and those things just come out."

Incidentally, on the song "Woman", which became the B-side of "Leave Me Be", there is a whole set of similar kinds of scales running up and down, provided simultaneously by the bass, the guitar and the electric organ. A positive love song with a lyric somewhat in the same mould as The Beatles' "I Should Have Known Better" (from *A Hard Day's Night*), this is otherwise a pretty straight forward rhythm 'n' blues song featuring solos from both guitar and organ. It isn't exactly the group's most exhilarating recording, yet it comes across considerably better than the rhythm 'n' blues covers they were soon to lay down for their first LP. Furthermore, the official version has the benefit of being liberated from a pretty odd-sounding bridge which was featured on the demo.

Generally, The Zombies already sounded tougher and more self-assured, not just compared with the demo session two weeks earlier, but also compared with the very first session at Decca. For some reason, Terry Johnson once again had his drumsticks out for the mix-down of "Woman"; otherwise Hugh Grundy reigns supreme on the rhythm front. Since the last recording session he had bought himself a superb Ludwig drum kit (the same brand as Ringo Starr's); Chris White had got himself a Gibson bass which he would continue to use throughout the Decca period, and Paul Atkinson was trying out a new semi-acoustic guitar:

"I got a Gretsch Chet Atkins, which was a double cut-away. It's a great guitar, but I ended up not liking it very much. I couldn't get a great tone out of it. In retrospect I should have got the Country Gentleman, which is the George Harrison one. It has a much more cutting tone."

It appears that on these recordings Atkinson resorted to his acoustic Zenith with its magnetic pick-ups. Rod Argent, on the other hand, had purchased himself a Vox Continental electric organ which was very much featured during the session.

"I have mixed feelings about the Vox organ," Argent reckons today. "I enjoyed having it at the time. It was great on stage, 'live'. Looking back on it, I think the sound of the Vox organ dates a lot more, generally speaking, than the Pianette. The Pianette still sounds great to me in its period fashion, whereas against the Hammond C3 or B3 the Vox sounds very weedy, although I must say you can still listen to The Animals' 'House Of The Rising Sun' – it still sounds great on that."

One of the problems with Vox organs is that they are very limited; for instance they sound good only with the vibrato turned on. They come across as very synthetic, prompting me in some other connection to describe their sound as the equivalent of the taste you get from "chewing on a Lego brick" (being Danish born and bred what else would be at the forefront of my imagination?) More prosaically, they demand a very particular style of soloing, where the musician plays variations on chords rather than single notes. Rod Argent had figured out this technique by the time of "What More Can I Do" (the B-side of the group's third single), but during the "Leave Me Be" session he still seems a bit in the dark about how to use the instrument and it would probably have been a better option at the time if he had just stayed with the Pianette (on stage, he would from now on use both keyboards, piling the Pianette on top of the organ).

All in all, the band's recollections of their second Decca session aren't too happy:

"I remember rehearsing 'Leave Me Be' at Paul's parents' house," said Chris White, "and it really sounded good. We

Above: The Zombies taking time off from touring to study classic architecture, 1964. (l-r) Hugh Grundy, Paul Atkinson, Chris White, Colin Blunstone and Rod Argent. *Photo: RB.*

Above: The Zombies in sombre mood, 1964.

Below: The Zombies say nope to dope, 1964. *Photos: RB.*

Above: Competition-winning Zombies take a guitar lesson from pre-platform Shane Fenton (a.k.a. Alvin Stardust). *Photo: Gems.*
Below: A new image, 1966. Suits out, sweaters in. (l-r) Hugh Grundy, Paul Atkinson, Chris White, Rod Argent, Colin Blunstone, *Photo: RB.*

Above: A collector's dream. The Zombies worldwide appeal led to singles and albums being sold in many different markets.

Opposite top: US dress code meets faithful Scandanavian audience as The Zombies perform for Swedish television. *Photo: Michael Ochs Archive.*

Opposite bottom: Rod Argent predicted progressive rock by half a decade by stacking keyboard instruments on stage. *Photo: Michael Ochs Archive.*

Briefly back from the grave: The Zombies reunion, Jazz Café, London, 1998.

Above: (l-r) Blunstone, White, Argent, Atkinson, Grundy.

Left: Paul Atkinson and Rod Argent compare notes.

Below: Classic British drummer Hugh Grundy still going strong.

More 1998 reunion shots,
Jazz Café, London, 1998.

Top left: Chris White.
Above: Paul Atkinson.
Top right: Colin Blunstone.
Middle right: The Zombies with
faithful fans.
Bottom right: Good to be back
on stage!

All reunion photos: Mick Hutson.

Above: How it all started, The Zombies happy to be No 1, 1964.
Photo: Harry Goodwin.

were really disappointed with the recording of it, because the voice was so whispery. It sounded great 'live', but Ken Jones wanted Colin to sing wispy and it lost its edge, and also we had to come down by train overnight, because we were on a tour, and record in the morning. That's never a good thing for a voice."

Rod Argent also recalls Ken Jones' attempting to recreate the success of "She's Not There" by drawing on the same qualities that he felt had made the first song a hit. In those days, where even The Beatles expressed doubts that their popularity would last for more than a couple of years, record producers were often thinking in such narrow-minded ways. If you had a hit, the idea was to make the next record sound exactly the same.

Ken Jones' philosophy that The Zombies' commercial potential mainly lay in Blunstone's hushed voice on "She's Not There" seems a very bad analysis indeed. What was much more essential to the song's success was the way it was arranged around a strong, easily recognisable riff. You only have to take a brief look at other beat group songs that made it big at the time, including The Beatles' records, to realise how important it was to have a strong hook or riff to base your songs on. In The Zombies' case, only two of their singles ever really had such a feature – "She's Not There" and "Time Of The Season". Both went to Number 1 in the US charts.

During their lifetime The Zombies made many records that were artistically on a par with their two big hits and sometimes, to my mind, better. However, in a commercial sense these songs lacked that "certain something", that instantly recognisable characteristic which could grasp the general public's short attention span.

From a purely musical point of view, however, such debate is irrelevant apart from the fact that deliberate attempts to be commercial occasionally can ruin otherwise good songs. That seems to be The Zombies' complaint over Ken Jones from "Leave Me Be" onwards. The only group member to have a different view on the matter, Hugh Grundy summed up the situation as follows, "You've got to blame somebody, so the poor old producers always get it in the neck."

Atypically, The Zombie's second single wasn't recorded in just one day. On 31 August the band managed only to lay down the backing tracks, then it was back out on the road. They returned on 5 September to add lead vocals and harmonies. This same procedure was also used on the other two tracks done at the time, "Sometimes" and "Kind Of Girl". Both are considerably more obscure Rod Argent compositions, being relegated to a rare EP issued in January the following year.

"Sometimes" opens with an *a cappella* introduction and then continues in a more basic rhythm 'n' blues mode. The main chord-change moves between D and alternatively G major and G minor.

As already mentioned, variations of this kind are a trademark of the group. Another kind of change that is akin to this is shifts between two major chords that are three semitones apart. Such changes appear in the songs of both Argent and White.

It would be interesting to know why the two writers had such an affection for these particular, somewhat unusual forms of chord progression. So I asked them, but found only that they were not even aware of these significant patterns which appear in nearly every song either of them has ever written for The Zombies!

My only explanation must be that they represent some kind of "young man's short-cut to sounding jazzy". It appears to me that if you like modern jazz but can't really make out what all the strange chords are on your Miles Davis records, you will end up with a set of basic chords moved around in a fashion that gets you as close to your idol as possible.

That may not sound particularly flattering, but in fact what could be seen as an inadequacy made for a completely unique style. As with the drum sound on "She's Not There" it was a blessing in disguise, because out of The Zombies' inability – and lack of ambition – to play jazz properly was born something that was entirely new and fresh.

"Rod in his solos would go places where other people wouldn't go," Chris White said to me. "But it's what he'd heard and what he'd been used to from listening to Miles Davis, and it's just being free with the music. We weren't playing improvisational jazz at all – we weren't capable of it."

However, what Rod Argent and Chris White *were* capable of was writing unusual chord sequences. These were simple when compared with modern jazz, nevertheless for a beat group they were highly sophisticated. The writers could go from such sequences straight into three-chord blues, then into classical inspirations from the Renaissance to the Impressionists and back again within the same song and without losing the plot on the way. Most important of all, on top of these chord sequences they would write flowing, beautiful melodic lines in the best of British tradition. Finally there were the lyrics, laments from a world where boys complained to other boys about how badly they had been hurt by cynical and unfathomable girlfriends.

Neither "Sometimes" nor "Kind Of Girl" belongs among the strongest performances the group ever delivered on record, yet both songs fit pretty well into the above description and very much signalled what lay ahead.

Being in the public limelight meant that the group had to develop some kind of an image. Unfortunately, it seemed that their promoter and record label didn't have many options to choose from. The only thing that seemed to set these guys apart from the mass of other groups popping up all over Britain at the time was the fact that they were slightly better educated than most.

It probably seemed like a good idea to begin with – a group that couldn't be written off by the establishment and the parent generation as scruffy, loud and rebellious. Hence The Zombies were promoted as a band that parents could point to and tell their offspring: look, you don't have to give up on good manners, clean fingernails and school just because you like beat groups!

It appears that the group initially had no problems with adapting to this, with Chris White proclaiming in *New Musical Express* that his biggest dislikes were "untidy, rude and unthinking people." In the longer run, however, it probably wasn't a very sound image at all to promote. Running through stacks of articles on the group during 1964-65 it is striking how practically every journalist feels the need to emphasize how clever, polite and well-educated this group are, something which has stuck with them to this very day and is often highly exaggerated (as late at November 1999 a reviewer in *Hi-Fi Choice* claimed that the band had 30 "A" levels between them).

Had The Zombies been sons of coal miners or dock workers, the majority of their countrymen might have taken to them. Even coming from a seemingly decadent upper-class environment could have been dangerously exciting (it worked for Marianne Faithfull). But being lower middle-class bordering on prosperous upper working-class, and having a history of mainly liking your parents and doing well at school wasn't what most youngsters craved when it came to rock 'n' roll, not even in the still-innocent early sixties. After all, being in a beat group was one of the few possibilities a working-class lad had of making it out of his drab home environment. The last thing you wanted was posh, over-confident Grammar School boys taking over that business as well!

Today, all this is probably of very little relevance. However, during my interviews I found Chris White, and particularly Rod Argent, eager to stress that in fact they came from working-class, not middle-class backgrounds. Paul Atkinson had a different view:

"When the other guys say we were working-class, I don't really think that's true. I think all of us were really middle-class. If you think about the bands that were coming down from Manchester and Liverpool and Sheffield, *these* were working-class bands. The Animals from Newcastle – these were working-class families. Unfortunately, we got tagged with this 'brainy' tag, which was a millstone around our neck. For some reason our publicists, either at Decca or otherwise, used to latch on to that. I regret that. Rock 'n' roll is supposed to be rebellious, and if you're a geek or a nerd and you're supposed to be brainy it's not exactly the rebellious rock 'n' roll, Rolling Stones-image. I think that really hurt us later on. The music that Rod wrote, and to a lesser extent the music that Chris wrote, was definitely sophisticated. It absolutely was. We were very proud of that. We didn't play it down. We thought this was our distinguishing feature – that and Colin's voice. We weren't trying to squelch that. But at the same time that sophisticated musicality coupled with the alleged brainy image, I do think that limited our audience."

This may all be true, but there were also audiences who themselves were doing decently at school and were interested in musical innovation. John DuCann, later the guitarist and singer with Atomic Rooster, was a fourteen year-old fan who managed to track down the band in a café in St Albans:

"I handed them their latest single to sign, which was 'Leave Me Be' at the time. I still think that was the best one they did – I love the minor chords and the breathy vocal [sic]. A very underrated record, I don't know why it didn't become a big hit. Anyway, they signed my record on the sleeve and they were very nice and friendly, but also seemed to be a bit taken aback by it all. It was as though they were wondering, 'Is this really us doing this – signing our autographs?'"

Another future first-class musician, Procol Harum's Matthew Fisher, who most famously played the haunting organ theme on "A Whiter Shade Of Pale", told me about his first encounter with The Zombies:

"I saw them play in Croydon in 1964. It was a big package tour with all sorts of people including The Searchers. I was certainly interested in The Zombies, though they might not have been the band I went to see. They were great. Colin was leaping around all over the place and very visual. The harmonies were fantastic. It was just a good show, generally. I always liked The Zombies' songs. The thing was, however, that you had this feeling about The Zombies that they were a rather intellectual group. So I was anticipating that kind of thing. I saw them as music for the more serious rock 'n' roll enthusiast. Did the Grammar School boy image hurt them? I don't know, it didn't do them any harm with me."

A third follower, Phil Smee, feels differently:

"Working-class kids who were into beat music would think, 'How can these people possibly know how to rock?' Not that they were well-off, but that's the way it seemed. It didn't do them any favour to get that 50 'O' levels tag. A lot was made of that. It just goes to show the mindset of the reviewers and writers at the time!"

11

Don't begin here

Autumn 1964 was the height of Beatlemania, and at times it could be quite dangerous for any pop group to walk the streets of the towns they were playing in. Trying to leave venues just after you had performed was even more of a worry. In The Zombies' case carrying your own amplifiers and instruments made it almost impossible to defend yourself against girls armed with scissors trying to cut a lock off their idol's hair.

At that time BBC Radio had a programme called *Jukebox Jury*, where a panel that included fellow musicians would judge newly released records. The week that "She's Not There" came out, George Harrison was on the panel and he said some very nice things about the single.

"He really liked it," Colin Blunstone recalled. "It was funny, because it all seems so easy when you're young. It all seemed a bit inevitable, somehow."

Though "She's Not There" stalled at Number 12 in the UK charts, and "Leave Me Be" (released on 16 October) wasn't even a minor hit, The Zombies got their share of the toils and troubles of being a group during the Beat Boom. However, this was all just a weak forerunner for what was about to happen.

There was a time when it didn't look as though the debut single was going to be released in America at all. But publisher Al Gallico was enthusiastic about it and made sure he got the rights for it. After that he started trying to persuade several US labels to release the record, and was eventually lucky to convince Walt McGuire of Parrot Records that there was a big potential here.

After some negotiation "She's Not There" was released by Parrot Records in the USA, the day after "Leave Me Be" had come out in the UK. It stormed into the charts on 17 October and things were looking very promising indeed, so much so that it was decided the group should start recording their first album right away.

This decision was built on a feeling among management and record labels of having to strike while the iron was hot. However, it wasn't a well-considered plan at all to take a small local UK band of teenagers, who had only one hit record to their credit, and try squeezing a full album out of them between doing gigs all over the country.

This is perhaps the area where Ken Jones most fatally misunderstood what was going on with the group. The Zombies weren't a brief success that had to be cashed in on as soon as possible before it disappeared again. If nurtured in the right manner, and with investment in the form of studio time and creativity, they could have been a phenomenon that would go on for years and play a very important part in a musical revolution. Unfortunately, this was not to happen.

To make everything even more tense, the band had a Scandinavian tour coming up, their first visit abroad.

Work on what would eventually become the LP *Begin Here* commenced on 24 November at Decca's No. 2 studio in West Hampstead following two months fully-booked with one night stands and TV appearances. In fact, the group on several occasions found themselves playing two gigs a night!

On the first day of recording, The Zombies put down cover versions of three R&B songs, "I'm Going Home", "Road Runner" and "Sticks And Stones", before hurrying off to participate in the filming of the *Red Skelton Show*.

"Road Runner" was a Bo Diddley song which the band used to open their shows.

"We used to quite enjoy that," Blunstone said. "We did lots of songs like that, especially when we were amateurs, which other groups also used to do. The audiences liked it. I enjoyed singing that song, but I don't think the recorded track is one of our finest moments."

Another favourite of the group, and of Rod Argent in particular, was "I'm Going Home". I'm not sure I quite agree with him here, and it doesn't seem that Ken Jones did either. The song went straight into the Decca vaults and never saw the light of day until a compilation LP in 1984.

The following day no fewer than seven tracks were laid down all in one go; all new, self-composed material. These songs were Rod Argent's "Tell Her No", "I Remember When I Loved Her", "I Want You Back Again", "The Way I Feel Inside" (group version) and "Walking In The Sun"; the remaining two tracks were written by Chris White and titled "What More Can I Do" and "I Don't Want To Know".

"It was perhaps a bit rushed in the studio," Hugh Grundy recalled. "It's all about the money. They say, 'Well, you've got this time. If you go over, it's going to cost you this, cost you that.' They're forever putting you under pressure. I think we were pretty good in the studio. We were well-rehearsed. I think that kept down studio costs enormously. Lots of other groups would experiment. You look at The Beatles; they went on forever. They would try different instruments, sounds and so on. We did too, to a certain extent, but that was with the later stuff. To begin with you haven't got the luxury of doing that. It was all done on four tracks and bounced down to one, with bits and pieces added on top and not a lot more."

Surprisingly the new, self-written material worked much better than the rhythm 'n' blues covers recorded on the previous day, though the latter category of songs had been performed by the band on stage for a very long time. In fact these covers form a "dark chapter" in the group's career and are, particularly when played in succession with their own compositions, almost unbearable to listen to. The band somehow manages to sound over-zealous and feeble at the same time, but even worse it appears that Colin Blunstone doesn't really know what to do with his voice. He wavers up and down, seemingly trying to elaborate on the melodies by phrasing in the same manner as Manfred Mann's Paul Jones would do, ignoring the fact that their voices are very dissimilar and call for very different deliveries.

"I thought Manfred Mann were sensational," Blunstone confirmed to me. "Before we became professional I went to see them at the Marquee, and I thought they were great. I really did. But I had an awful lot of learning to do as a singer. I'm still learning now. Then, I was very raw and sometimes it was apparent."

Again, it very much counts against Ken Jones that he didn't at least give the group enough time and guidance in the studio to get these songs right (or alternatively just scrap them). As a producer, he should have been the first to recognise that there was a major problem. The band themselves, worn-out by touring and rushed along, had no control whatsoever over the proceedings.

"When Colin did 'Sticks And Stones' he might not even have heard the play-through," Rod Argent told me. "It might have been, 'No, that's great guys, on to the next one.' Whereas if we'd been making demos ourselves we would have listened to it and Colin would have said, 'Ah, I think I'll do that again.'"

To put it bluntly, the rhythm 'n' blues covers recorded for the first Zombies LP ought never to have seen the light of day, not even retrospectively. Nevertheless, on the 1997 box set *Zombie Heaven* they are still being allowed to ruin the whole first disc (titled "Begin Here & Singles").

Rather than dwell any more on this, let us look at the self-written songs recorded on the following day, which are an absolute delight. First and foremost there is Argent's "Tell Her No", which became the group's third single by January the following year.

Unsurprisingly, it features one boy warning another that his girlfriend – whom he loves very much – is totally unreliable, immoral and unpredictable. There is a good chance she will soon approach the friend and try to win him over with her charms and promises of love. Consequently, the narrator takes the precaution to warn his friend and advises him to "tell her no". In fact, the word "no" is repeated a legendary 70+ times during the track's brief two minutes and two seconds.

Only the lyric's deep-felt panic manages to save it from self-ridicule. However, it is on the musical front that things get truly interesting.

"Burt Bacharach was writing a lot of stuff around that time," Rod Argent recalled, "and there were 9th and 13th chords [basic chords augmented with extra notes] on that which were quite unusual in pop music, but Bacharach was using them. I seem to remember having heard the Dionne Warwick stuff, and it was coloured chords, and at least some of it was drinking in that atmosphere."

This statement is backed by the fact that The Zombies had been touring with Dionne Warwick around the time when Argent wrote the song. Chris White recalls that Rod in fact was trying deliberately to copy some augmented chords that he had heard in Burt Bacharach songs, but got them wrong, thus once again ending up with something uniquely his own.

"I remember the middle eight was the first thing I wrote away from the keyboard. I wrote it just in my head, with chords and melody and everything," Rod Argent continued. "I really liked the way it turned out."

Another noteworthy feature on the record, which happened purely by accident, was the slightly slurred lead vocals:

"I actually fell asleep while they were doing the backing tracks," Colin Blunstone admitted. "We were on the road all the time and I was just tired. They woke me up to sing 'Tell Her No'. I woke up, and I was a bit sleepy when I sang it. That's why there's a line in there that's mumbo-jumbo, really. So I said, 'Let's do that again.' But the producer said, 'It's fine, it's fine.' If you listen to it, it doesn't mean anything. Of course, that went to Number 6 in the States with me half asleep singing it!"

A beautiful and original arrangement featuring some excellent playing from all the band, particularly some delicate and innovative syncopated drumming from Hugh Grundy, "Tell Her No" was put down on the master tape with lead vocals and harmonies on the same track, drums and bass on another track, and guitar and piano on each of the remaining two tracks. This procedure would subsequently make for an almost half-decent stereo mix, though there is an urgency and presence on the original mono record which can't be replicated. I asked Chris White if the reason for this slight detour on the engineering front came about because Ken Jones was starting to think in terms of possible stereo mixes. "Definitely not," he said. "In those days we only ever planned for mixing in mono."

Something exciting happened during these recordings. The band received a phone call from America telling them that "She's Not There" was now Number 1 in the charts.

Chris White: "You can't believe what that meant. The second English [beat] group after The Beatles to have a Number 1 in America! Until The Beatles, America didn't know there was any such thing as English music. It felt unreal, like we were in a film. Still, we had to finish the session. Work, work, work. Part of our Protestant work ethos!"

Recorded during the same prolific session, White's "What More Can I Do" made it on to the B-side of "Tell Her No".

Colin Blunstone: "I just remember lots of words and having a bit of trouble fitting them all in. Chris often wrote songs like that. I probably complained about it. I probably needed to work on the phrasing a bit better. Without changing the song I think you could probably phrase it better than I did. But again at that time, because we got that hit 'She's Not There', I think often the recordings were done quite quickly. They had to be. Songs would be written one day and recorded the next. So sometimes some of them weren't done in the best way they could be."

"What More Can I Do" opens with a brief organ introduction presenting the main theme, an emulation of the classic Hit-the-Road-Jack descending chord progression. This also runs underneath the first two stanzas, then – in typical Chris White style – the song goes its own way with complete disregard to the accepted way of combining chords in songwriting, using the melody line to keep things together (rather than the norm of using so-called *leading notes* in the chords and movements in the bass line).

As with so many other Zombies songs the frustration and suspense in the lyrics is brilliantly reflected in arrangement and performance. Here we have the narrator complaining about his own inhibitions which prevent him from show-ing his girlfriend his true feelings (a much more defensive attitude towards the kind of debate which also appeared in "You Make Me Feel Good"), his desperation mirrored by some wild soloing from both organ and guitar. The song has been criticised for having too many words, but really it is just being played too fast by the group – something it would obviously have been Ken Jones' job to correct.

Though there are some surprising similarities between the songwriting of Rod Argent and Chris White, there is also at least one major difference in their approach to writing lyrics. Where Argent at this early stage had a tendency to state more-or-less everything he wanted to say in the first verse and chorus and subsequently just repeat the same mes-sage, reusing as many phrases as possible with just a varia-tion on a word or two, Chris White was able to spread his messages much more evenly throughout his songs. Colin Blunstone:

"I think of the two songwriters Rod certainly went for the sound of words and how it scanned, as much as what it meant. That was always my impression. I think Chris did often tell real stories in his songs."

It isn't easy to say which is the better method of writing. Perhaps Rod Argent's lyrics were more musical, but then Chris White's had an urgency that could win the listener over and certainly works better on paper.

In the other Chris White song recorded during that same session, "I Don't Want To Know", we start getting the suspicion that he and Rod Argent might at some point have had the same girlfriend. Certainly the floosie portrayed here has strong similarities with the girl in Argent's "Tell Her No", though in this case the narrator isn't warning his friend – he is the one being warned. You could say that "Tell Her No" represents one part of a conversation, while "I Don't Want To Know" represents the other. A lack of communication between all parties involved appears to be the underlying subject matter.

Musically, the recording belongs in the weaker part of the group's production. There is a nice guitar riff reminiscent of The Searcher's version of "When You Walk In The Room" (perhaps not coincidentally; the groups had just been touring together), but somehow it seems as if too much energy is being put into the performance, the subtle plot being lost somewhere along the way. A tougher, more solid attempt would probably have worked better – but time was scarce.

Introduced by simple but exquisitely executed acoustic guitar playing, Rod Argent's "I Remember When I Loved Her" picks up lyrically from "She's Not There". The song has an immensely beautiful melody line and introduces a kind of chord opening that would be much more natural for a guitarist to come up with than a keyboardist, giving a distinctive Spanish feel that is emphasised by the use of tambourine and various accentuations throughout the arrangement. The key is rather low for the Colin Blunstone we know so far, giving him a chance to display his impressive range. There is a ghostly organ solo with more ambience than you get in a cathedral, once again adding an almost morbid feel to the narrator's description of his former loved one. The track could have been a single but got relegated to Side 2 of the LP.

Even less lucky was "Walking In The Sun", which for many years ended up on a shelf somewhere in Decca's offices.

With this particular song Rod Argent embarked on a route of composing songs that had already outgrown the beat group format and called for much more elaborate arrangements.

It is tragic that Ken Jones didn't pick up on this quality and immediately started working as an orchestral arranger together with Rod Argent, the way that George Martin was soon to do with The Beatles. Not until December 1969, after The Zombies had long folded, was former Manfred Mann member Mike Vickers trusted with the original backing track for "Walking In The Sun", to which he added a stunning orchestral arrangement (at the same time as Blunstone redid his vocal). By then the song had been left in the vaults for four years, and it was to wait a lot longer until it finally came out in 1973, with the original unoverdubbed recording remaining unreleased until the 1997 box set.

Of a more naked beauty was "The Way I Feel Inside", which the group tried to record on the same day but failed to get right. Instead of finding out exactly what the problem was (the guitar playing a chord that collided with the melody line), the song was later attempted in a near *a cappella* version, which also ended up on *Begin Here*.

Finally there was "Somebody Help Me", another recording which wasn't considered successful. A new attempt was made during March the following year, but the first version nevertheless ended up on an American compilation LP called "Early Days", seemingly owing to a mistake by the record company.

Perhaps it needs to be repeated that these seven tracks, several of them pure classics, were all recorded by the group on the same day, probably during two three-hour sessions. Two days later The Zombies found themselves on a plane over the North Sea heading for Scandinavia.

12

Home and away

Colin Blunstone recalls the events surrounding the trip fondly: "The first time we went abroad with the band, we went to Norway. To be absolutely honest, if we walked down the road we stopped the traffic. I know it sounds bizarre and I think a lot of it was just to do with the length of our hair, and then you look back and it wasn't really long at all. It was just a new thing, and I'm not just saying that for Norway. It was new everywhere. Believe me, we didn't walk down the street that much, but when we walked to the bus or if we sat in the foyer of the hotel the whole window of the hotel was just completely blocked up with people staring at us. It was quite strange. We then went quickly to Finland and also to Sweden."

For the parents sending their young sons to these foreign shores, one aspect was particularly worrying.

"I had never been on a plane before," Hugh Grundy said.

"My father was an aircraft engineer and it frightened the poor guy to death!"

This brief tour formed the basis of a long love-affair between the group and particularly the youth of Sweden – The Zombies later issued a full album in this country which wasn't released anywhere else (though all the material was). In Norway they also seem to have maintained their popularity, while in Denmark they never really caught on, perhaps because their visit there during the first Scandinavian tour was for one day only. Interestingly, there is a rule of thumb in the music industry that Sweden is the only country in the world, except for Japan, where songs in minor keys regularly become hits; perhaps another reason why The Zombies went down so well there.

The band returned to England on 8 December. They had one day's rest, and found themselves back in the studio again the following day putting down six more tracks, "Can't Nobody Love You", "The Way I Feel Inside" (vocal/organ version), "I Got My Mojo Working" (featuring Rod Argent on lead vocals), "I Can't Make Up My Mind" (by Chris White), and finally an instrumental written by producer Ken Jones, titled "Work 'n' Play".

"I had a little chuckle there," Blunstone told me. "Our producer said, 'Oh, you've got to have an instrumental track on there – and I just happen to have written one!' I think there's a little bit of politics there."

Rod Argent added, "Ken was very keen to have one of his own compositions on the record. He was playing piano on that, and I played the harmonica."

Rod Argent's "The Way I Feel Inside" had, as mentioned, been attempted earlier; but there been certain problems with the arrangement and now it was re-recorded with Blunstone singing unaccompanied until the last verse, where the organ comes in. A stunning performance that underlined the singer's sublime talent and originality.

"That was another one written totally away from the keyboard," said Rod Argent. "It was actually written when we were on tour. We stopped somewhere, and strangely enough for a song with that title I wrote the whole song while I was on the toilet! When we got back to the bus afterwards, I just wrote it down on a piece of manuscript and that was it! When we recorded it I was amazed by how Colin managed to hold the pitch completely."

Unfortunately, the Vox organ featured at the end of "The Way I Feel Inside" sounds flat and wimpy; it would arguably have been better to just leave the voice completely on its own. Otherwise the song stands up beautifully in all its nakedness, though it could also have been interesting augmented with a string quartet. For someone with Ken Jones' qualifications and connections it would have been no problem to provide such an arrangement and a group of players for the occasion. However, this all happened before The Beatles had released "Yesterday" and to think in such innovative terms seemingly went beyond Jones' intentions with The Zombies.

While "The Way I Feel Inside" is about lacking the courage to speak about your feelings, Chris White's "I Can't Make Up My Mind" sees the narrator's former girlfriend suggesting they get back together, with him being desperate for someone to advise him. It is interesting for a relatively young person to write a song of this kind, with its pronounced references to domestic, married life. The prospect of returning "home" would regularly reappear in The Zombies' lyrics over years to come (as late as 1978 Rod Argent released a solo album titled *Moving Home*), a far cry from the let's-spend-the-night-together mentality normally associated with the 1960s. Another song with a somewhat Spanish feel to its chord progression, "I Can't Make Up My Mind" features a twelve-string electric guitar, something quite new in rock 'n' roll. Paul Atkinson:

"I got a Burns twelve-string, which could never stay in tune but it was all right for recordings. It was good, but it was very, very heavy. We did take it on the road to Sweden one time and it was very frustrating. It would go out of tune after one song. So I gave up and just used it on records."

"I Can't Make Up My Mind" has all The Zombies' high-quality trademarks, including some fine vocal harmonies from Argent and White. As on many of their other recordings it sounds as though three or more voices are performing the background vocals. Chris White:

"We were always puzzled why our vocals worked so well. You can't say why, but there's a certain clarity there. I'm not a great singer at all, and Rod used to give me very simple harmonies to do, but it's something that's quite strange. A lot of it's luck, anyway."

Colin Blunstone added, "Chris has got a very interesting sounding voice, especially when it's recorded. He sounds quite like John Lennon when he sings. He will always joke about his voice, but he's good.

"We did our harmonies in a strange way. I didn't come from a musical background, so often when there was a three-part harmony I'd get confused as to what was the melody and what was the harmony part. So Rod would say, 'You sing what you think is the melody.' Then, because Chris had to both play the bass and sing, Rod would try and give Chris a very simple harmony. It might almost be one note, or two or three notes. That would leave Rod filling out all the holes, which would often be incredibly complicated. But it gave the harmonies a unique feel. No one else did harmonies like that. With us, no one would be singing top or bottom harmony, because we were changing all the time. Rod was all over the place. I was singing most of the melody, but sometimes I would be singing the top harmony. And Chris was always singing in the middle somewhere. I think it gave it a very distinctive feel."

The remaining tracks laid down on this day – four more rhythm 'n' blues covers – all suffer from the same problems as earlier recordings of the same kind of material. Perhaps the medley of "You Really Got A Hold On Me"/"Bring It On Home To Me" works slightly better than the rest, but compared with the two self-written songs from the same session it's really not worth spending much time on. Once again, the time pressure was enormous.

"There was one song I always loved doing on stage," recalled Rod Argent, "which was 'I Got My Mojo Working'. When we did it in the studio I just tried something with my voice and I hated it. I went back into the control room and I said, 'Okay, I'm going to do it again.' But Ken said, 'No no, we're keeping it.' I was stuck with it! He wouldn't let me do it again. In those days it was once through and, 'Yeah, great!' It becomes very hit and miss."

Very much in the same manner, Colin Blunstone told me about the song "Can't Nobody Love You": "Again, we were short on songs. That's one I spotted on a Solomon Burke album in the morning, and I think we recorded it in the afternoon!"

Luckily, most of the remaining days up to Christmas 1964 were reasonably restful for the band. They made an appearance on BBC 2's *Open House*, and recorded a session for *Easy Beat*, a radio broadcast. Then, on 23 December, they flew to New York.

"'She's Not There' was Number 1 when we were over there playing the *Murray the K. Show* in New York," Colin Blunstone recalled. "I think once we played two songs, but mostly we only played that one song. There were fifteen or sixteen acts who all went on playing their one song, and that was that. There was a backing band for a lot of the American bands, and then there was the Nashville Teens doing 'Tobacco Road', us, and a band called The Hullabaloos. On the bill were The Shangrilas, Dionne Warwick, Ben E. King, The Shirelles, Patti La Belle & the Bluebells."

After the shows, the group was told that they couldn't venture out into the streets of New York, the reason being that they would be attacked by girl fans. Nevertheless, Paul Atkinson sneaked out via a back door declaring to the others, "This is silly. I'm going out." Immediately a huge crowd of girls ripped his shirt off him and pushed him up against a plate-glass window.

"They were only trying to be friendly," claimed Colin Blunstone, "but it's the weight of people that frightens you. Anyway, the police came and got him out. They said, 'Look. We got you out once, but we're not doing it again.' But the funny thing was, we used to hang around at the end while everyone went home. There was a bar next door and we'd go and have a beer. Then we'd go on the subway and go back to our hotel. People couldn't believe it because not only were we the Number 1 band in America at the time, it was also in Brooklyn, which is a fairly tough neighbourhood. Most Americans wouldn't go on the tube in Brooklyn late at night, but we used to. It was a bit weird that we wouldn't go out all day, and yet we'd have to walk down two or three blocks to get on the subway to get back to our hotel."

Paul Atkinson wasn't the only Zombie to be taken aback by the new environment. Hugh Grundy and Chris White recalled a frightening experience one day in Times Square where they had gone sight-seeing together with one of the other British groups on the bill, The Nashville Teens.

"Someone was shot in front of us – murdered," Chris White told me. "There were spent cartridges. The police came up and took them away. So New York was a big shock for us. We came from gentle, what people then considered as middle-class families, to see the chaos and hear the gunfire in New York. It was just like that television programme I used to watch, *The Naked City*."

The Zombies' first US visit was originally planned to be a tour going through January, but it didn't materialise because of problems with getting work permits. At least their temporary visas allowed them to play the radio shows at the Brooklyn Fox, and immediately after two TV shows, *Hullabaloo* and *Shindig*.

Paul Atkinson: "We came in the day before Christmas Eve to the Brooklyn Fox. We opened on Christmas Day. It was a very bizarre set-up, at least to us. You had all these bands and all these artistes, all of us doing one or two songs each. Basically you play your hit record and you get off. We would play five shows a day, occasionally six, and in between the shows they'd show a movie. It was actually very good value for money. Some of the kids would come out from one show and then stand in line for the next show the whole day. They'd see five shows in a row. Murray The K. was the host and the headliner was Chuck Jackson. It was a big TV variety show. We were the special guests from England.

"The show started with this big opening number where we all had to get on stage and link arms, a big number with an orchestra. Then everyone would leave and Murray would stick with the audience. He'd introduce the first act, and they would come on and do their one hit and they'd get off, then the next one and so forth. We would follow Patti LaBelle & the Bluebells. They always tore the house down because they did an amazing version of 'Danny Boy'. That was one of their big hits, and also 'You'll Never Walk Alone'. There was always a joke between us as they were coming into the wings and we'd be waiting to go on – they'd all giggle and say, 'Follow that!' It was very difficult, because the audience was mostly black and they were huge favourites. But we did okay, because we were English. We went out there and it was all screams, of course, and no one could really hear us. So we got away with it."

For Atkinson in particular, this New York visit would prove decisive for the future. His wife-to-be, Molly Molloy, was a dancer on the Murray The K. show:

"There was a couple of dancers on the show, one blonde and one brunette," he recalled. "I don't know what happened, but one thing led to another and I started dating Molly. We corresponded. The Zombies came back for a tour later that spring and she flew out to wherever we were, and then later on she moved to England in 1966. We sort of carried on, and we got married in '67, as the group was breaking up. I was very young. I was eighteen years old. She was 24 and she'd just got divorced. My parents were a bit shocked about that. Their teenager was carrying on with a divorced American woman!"

When The Zombies returned to the UK in mid-January, one of their members had particular reasons for feeling worn-out. Rod Argent:

"I was very tired when we came back from the States. At that time you used to have to have all sorts of injections to go to America, including small pox injections which reacted very badly with me. I remember going there with jet lag, doing six shows a day at the Brooklyn Fox and I had huge ulcers in my throat. I felt really ill. I didn't feel well at all on that first visit to America, so I was pretty drained when I got back."

Luckily for Argent, the remaining part of January was more relaxed. Not only had the US tour been dropped, a tour of South Africa with Dusty Springfield was cancelled as well.

In the meantime, "Tell Her No" had been released in the States on 2 January 1965 (coupled with "Leave Me Be", which had not previously come out in America). The UK release came later, on 29 January. On that same day the group's one-and-only British EP was released. Despite the inclusion of the magnificent "Summertime", the EP sank without a trace (making it a highly-collectable item later on), while "Tell Her No" at least reached Number 42 in the British charts.

By now, it was becoming more and more obvious that The Zombies' audience was mainly to be found on the other side of the Atlantic where, within less than a fortnight, "Tell Her No" had gone to Number 6 in both the *Cashbox* and *Billboard* charts.

To coincide with the (later cancelled) US tour in January, Parrot had a US album planned for release as well. For some reason things got held up, and it appears that the record wasn't in the shops until the following month. Sales were initially rather slow. That, however, mattered less now that the tour was cancelled anyway. Despite its thrown-together nature and some copies being in horrible-sounding "reprocessed stereo", the LP – simply titled *The Zombies* – roamed the US charts for a healthy seventeen weeks, peaking at Number 39.

From February onwards the band were back in the routine of racing up and down the British mainland playing one-nighters, interrupted by radio and TV appearances. Nevertheless, 2 February was devoted entirely to a photo session for Decca. Unfortunately, the result somehow came out rather like an optician's advertisement.

"In those days your first photos seemed to stay with you forever," Colin Blunstone recalled. "Ours were awful, and that was another unfortunate thing. They stuck with us for the whole of our career."

On 2 March, four tracks were laid down at Decca's West Hampstead Studios No. 2, namely "Somebody Help Me" (second attempt), Chris White's composition "I Must Move", Rod Argent's "She's Coming Home", and Colin Blunstone's first stab at songwriting, "Just Out Of Reach".

It appears that with "She's Coming Home" Ken Jones at least partly recognised the kind of material Rod Argent was writing at this point. These were "big songs" calling for elaborate arrangements, songs that could easily have been covered by artists such as Dusty Springfield or Tom Jones while still retaining that magical Beat Boom feel.

By now, it wasn't too unusual to let beat groups break the combo formula by working with orchestras; even The Paramounts, who had a much lower commercial status than The Zombies, recorded "Blue Ribbons"/"Cuttin' In" for Parlophone with an orchestral group around the same time. Argent and his friends were not so lucky. Instead of augmenting the group, all Ken Jones managed to come up with was a ridiculous amount of reverb, drowning out the recording of a truly excellent song and performance.

Argent's composition introduces into his own idiom at least two important features which would later become trademarks of the group, and which both are about releasing the bass lines from the strict role of just playing root notes. Firstly, during the entire opening stanza the bass remains on the same note, while the chords above it change (something Chris White had also experimented with on "I Don't Want To Know"). Secondly, this is followed by a short descending bass line leading into the chorus.

Another feature which should be mentioned is Argent's use of a diminished chord (something he had started working with on "The Way I Feel Inside" and "I Remember When I Loved Her").

Finally, "She's Coming Home" varies somewhat from

standard pop song structure by retaining the opening chord sequence during the second line of the last verse, instead of following the structure established in the first verse where the aforementioned descending bass line is incorporated (this form of variation was also used by Chris White in "What More Can I Do").

"'She's Coming Home' was based on a composition called *Magnificat And None Nunc Dimittis* by Herbert Howell that we used to sing in the choir," Argent said. "The *Nunc Dimittis* I always remember thinking was really bluesy, and I nicked the chord sequence to form the basis of 'She's Coming Home'."

The lyric rejoices in the narrator's girlfriend's declaration that she intents to return "home" (once again the domestic element). As in most other early Zombies songs, the male part of the relationship seems pretty defenceless; like a ship at sea he is tossed about by circumstance and completely at the mercy of her everchanging moods. "I don't think we were ever remotely macho," Chris White said to me. I believe he is right. Even when he himself, in "I Must Move", partly builds on the classic "lone ranger" theme, there is very little Wild West hero about him. Instead, his declaration of inability ever to stay in one place long is soft-spoken, apologetic. In accordance with this, the chord sequence is superdense, full of major-to-minor shifts.

Unfortunately, during the mix Ken Jones once again went overboard with the reverb control, a problem that gets even worse if you listen the compact disc versions. (With analogue sound there is a loss of reverb with every generation copy – to get from master tape to someone's domestic Hi-Fi the music must undergo at least three generations of copying. Hence producers and engineers in the sixties would always put a lot of reverb on mixes, knowing that some 50 percent would disappear on the way. With digital sound there is no such loss, and hence sixties music on compact disc – lifted straight from the original mastertapes – often sounds as though far too much reverb has been used; yet another reason not to part with your original vinyl.)

Recorded on the same day, Colin Blunstone's thoroughly convincing debut as a songwriter, "Just Out Of Reach", is straightforward rhythm 'n' blues. The intention was that the song be included in a film, *Bunny Lake Is Missing*, in which The Zombies were also supposed to appear (which they did – for about 30 seconds on a TV screen in a restaurant).

"We were contracted to do three songs for the film," recalls Colin Blunstone, "and Rod hadn't got any. But it happened that I got a slight idea, and I managed to sort of build it up into a song. It was a case of 'necessity is the mother of invention' really. Again it was recorded in a big rush. In my desperation to write this song as quickly as possible I remembered my favourite song on the Nina Simone album *Live At The Town Hall* called 'Wild As The Wind'. Well, 'Just Out Of Reach' started out as 'Wild As The Wind', because I couldn't think of a title!"

The song's punchy approach forms a nice contrast to Argent and White's more pensive contributions around the same time. However, other features suggest that Blunstone had let himself be inspired by the group's two chief songwriters as there is a D major to F major chord-change during the brief chorus (akin to a major-minor change), and the lyric unsurprisingly requests the narrator's loved one to return "home". The rhythm guitar sounds delicious crisp and is played with Atkinson's typical good taste and robust feel, while the Vox organ solo is sheer bliss.

"Just Out Of Reach" coupled with Chris White's "Remember You" would end up as B-side and A-side, respectively, of arguably the group's strongest release since "She's Not There". Unfortunately, nearly a year had passed by in the meantime, and when it finally came out on 21 January 1966 it was received with indifference.

In fact, "Remember You" is a song so original and intriguing that it must stand out as one of the very best in the group's entire catalogue. "I first had the idea for that at Winston Churchill's funeral," Chris White recalled. "I heard the bagpipes playing, and I thought, 'That's the beginning of a nice phrase.' So I used it and I did it in 6/8."

Starting out with a simple two-chord riff the song suddenly employs an unusual descending chord progression, leading into an even more unorthodox chorus with constant shifts between the familiar and the innovative. As with so many other Zombies songs, the melody line, which keeps it all together, is so beautiful that the song could easily have stood up as an instrumental.

All in all, The Zombies' three-hour session for Decca on 2 March 1965 was successful in the sense that it produced no fewer than three single A-sides and two B-sides.

Apart from the already mentioned four tracks, "Somebody Help Me" in its new recording showed that the group were indeed capable of playing some very fine R&B, particularly when they had their own names down as songwriters. Another great performance that became a lost opportunity, the song could have graced the band's first album. Instead its title was changed to "I Want You Back Again" and was released as a single in the US only on 25 June, coupled with the UK album track "I Remember When I Loved Her".

The same single came out in Australia, but the only European release of the A-side track was on a French EP. The reason for not releasing the song in Britain might have been that it was intended Johnny Kidd and the Pirates should do a version of it. This seems never to have happened, and certainly nothing was released.

On 8 March a minor change occurred, which nevertheless

transformed the group's entire image – Paul Atkinson went to an optician to substitute his horn-rimmed specs with a pair of contact lenses.

"I couldn't wait to get rid of the glasses," he told me. "I hated wearing them. I had very, very near sight and my glasses were very thick. I wasn't trying to emulate Buddy Holly or anything, I wore them because I *had* to wear them! I was blind without them. As soon as I could save up £60, or whatever it was, I got contact lenses. Then the problem was, 'Who's your new guitar player?' 'Well, it's the same guy!' I went back to America in April for the next tour, and some of the American kids said, 'Well, what's your name?' I said, 'Oh, it's the same as it was before.' But I was much happier not wearing glasses."

The group were back in the studio on 31 March to record an alternative – and inferior – version of "Remember You" only to be used in the film soundtrack, and a new Chris White song called "Nothing's Changed".

The latter, a song about meeting a former girlfriend and discovering your feelings for her are unchanged, is seemingly a simple little pop song, yet closer scrutiny reveals an enticingly flowing structure in both words and music. Unfortunately, the otherwise impeccable performance is somewhat let down by Blunstone's vocal delivery being so breathy and intimate it borders on parody. The group once again claim their innocence and point to Ken Jones as the guilty party.

"Nothing's Changed" first came out on a 1965 Decca compilation LP called *14* (a highly-collectable record also known as *The Lord Tavener LP*, including rare tracks by The Rolling Stones, Them and others). The song also ended up on the soundtrack for *Bunny Lake Is Missing*.

Finally, recorded on the same day, was an alternative vocal track for Blunstone's "Just Out Of Reach" meant only to be used in the trailer for the film and encouraging audiences to "Come On Time"!

The film's director, Otto Preminger, was present at some of these recordings but was not a popular person with the group. "Very difficult man, the director," Blunstone told me. "God, he was atrocious. It's not just me saying that, he was renowned for it."

On 9 April "She's Coming Home"/"I Must Move" was released in the UK but hardly made any impact on home audiences (it went to Number 48 in the US *Cashbox* charts). On the same day, the band's first UK album also hit the shops. It didn't win them many new friends either.

John DuCann: "I had started listening to bands like The Yardbirds by then, who had a really solid and punchy approach. Compared with this The Zombies didn't impress me much in the rhythm 'n' blues department."

"I heard the LP over at a friend's place," Les Lambert recalled. "All these weak R&B covers. I thought, 'Oh no, this isn't for me.' I liked the keyboards, but I'd heard Jimmy Smith and things like that and I was much keener on the sound of the Hammond. My own band had done some gigs with Georgie Fame at the end of '62 and compared to that Vox organs and Farfisas and Pianettes and things like that were just wimpy, silly noises. I didn't think much of that."

Even devotees like Matthew Fisher, who rushed out and bought the LP, are somewhat reluctant to praise it:

"The Zombies were very much a singles band, mainly because that was the era they came out in. Album bands hadn't been invented yet, so to speak. I thought the first album was interesting but I don't think that there was anything on it that was as good as the singles. It was an album, as it were. But it was interesting. I certainly wasn't disappointed. For the time, it was great. It wasn't just a collection of singles."

13

Lucky stars

The Zombies' second US visit started in late April 1965 when they joined the Dick Clark Caravan of Stars.

Colin Blunstone: "We weren't on the tour for the first couple of days. We picked the tour up sort of halfway on the way down to the South. It was The Shangrilas again, we were always working with them. Del Shannon was on it, Tommy Roe, and Dee Dee Sharp and several more acts. Each of us only played one or two songs per night. Actually, Dee Dee Sharp drew a gun on someone. It got quite frisky on these buses sometimes. She had to leave the tour. They thought that wasn't very ladylike. There was a lot going on on that tour, no doubt about it."

The Zombies all state that they had never been seriously aware of racial conflicts before they toured the southern states of the USA (probably because there were no immigrants in St Albans – had the group come from certain parts of London they might have had different experiences).

"We couldn't eat in some restaurants," Blunstone recalled. "We couldn't stay at some hotels, and when we played big arenas you would see the toilets were segregated. It was quite a shock, because to a large extent our heroes were all black musicians, and we were touring with black musicians. There was nothing of that sort in England."

There are several stories about how the black acts participating in the Dick Clark Caravan Tour complimented the British group on their musical abilities and enjoyed hearing them perform black R&B covers. However, Blunstone painted a slightly bleaker picture of the same situation:

"I think maybe some of the black artists were getting fed up, because we were copying their records and having more success with them than they had. I can understand if they did, although no one ever said anything to me. Also some of the bands were being paid so little money. We weren't being paid very much either, and we only stayed in a hotel every second night. On alternate nights, we drove through the night. What seemed to happen to me was, we'd drive through the night and all the acts would sing. Especially the black acts would sing all the way through the night, and play music. Then the next night you'd get a hotel, but you want to go out to a party or something. So we really didn't get much sleep."

After the tour had made its way through the South it continued up through California to Canada. "That was great, although it was exhausting," Paul Atkinson said. "It was an amazing experience. We really saw the country from a Greyhound bus. Audience reception was incredible. We were totally spoiled."

At the end of the tour the band found themselves on their knees with fatigue. As a consequence, Paul Atkinson had lost a lot of weight and had to be collected from the airport, practically unconscious, by his parents.

"I like travelling," Blunstone stated, "but I like to take my time a bit more I think. It's not quite the same when you got to move on every day and you have no choice over where you're going."

Another problem, allegedly of a general nature, was that the band didn't earn as much money on the tour as they were promised.

Chris White: "We never received the money we should have. For one reason or another we did a six-week Dick Clark tour, playing every single night, sleeping every other night on the bus, with hit records, and we got £500 each for the whole six weeks!"

Though the band in general have fond memories of their US visits, there were frightening moments in between. As they were a British group, they were travelling in the wake of Beatlemania and hence exposed to their fair share of girl screaming hysteria.

"They would come at you with scissors and cut bits off your hair," recalled Chris White. "That was quite frightening. People said, 'Are you scared of girls?' We said, 'You haven't seen them!' They were very, very frightening. Often the screaming was so bad we couldn't hear ourselves playing. Remember, we were playing stadiums with Vox AC30s and no miking on the drums. Nobody cared, because they could hear the vocals. It was unbelievable. Pure hysteria. We were playing somewhere to 40-50,000 people, and Paul's amp went down so he plugged into my bass amp, and every time he took a solo the bass disappeared. It's crazy, but we went down a storm. A bit of magic at the time."

Colin Blunstone particularly recalls playing the Forum in Montreal. Another act appearing on the bill that night were

Herman's Hermits, who were exceptionally popular with young girl audiences at the time:

"When they went on stage, 10,000 people in the Forum all got up in one wave and came towards the stage. I thought, 'Hm. It might be time to have a little walk outside.' I didn't mind the girl screaming, though. It was pretty loud, but no one had a reaction like The Beatles had. And of course they were locked away in hotels. It was difficult for them. It was a little bit like that for us for a short period, but a lot of the time we were free to do whatever we wanted."

Hugh Grundy: "Now and again it was frightening. That's for sure. We were coming out of the theatre we were playing in Las Vegas. We'd done our spot. The idea was that when you'd finished your spot it was straight out of the back door, straight on to the bus and gone. But the bus was parked rather a long way away from the door, and by the time we were running out of the door the girls came rushing out the front and around the back. They were running towards us and I was last. One of them was obviously a better sprinter than I was. She caught up with me and got hold of my hair, and down I went. I was knocked unconscious. Absolutely. Fortunately the tour manager, a big guy called Frankie, was following up behind and he saw this had happened. He just picked me off the tarmac and threw me on the coach and away we went. Pretty frightening. I came to after that, a bit groggy. But to be a young man and to go and see America as we did, experience what we experienced, meet the people that we did, go to the parties – it was absolutely wonderful."

Returning home to Britain, where the band's status was considerably lower, could have the emotional effect of a cold shower.

Paul Atkinson: "On one hand going to America was wonderful, on the other hand it was very frustrating. We would come home to England and be nobodies. We'd be playing to 15,000 people in stadiums in America. Then we'd come home and we would play to 200 people in a club. I couldn't wait to go back to the States for the next tour, but the other source of frustration was that after 1965 we never did go back."

It may be that Atkinson's memories of returning home are bleaker than those of the other band members. It seems he still had precious little support from his family in his musical career, as Chris White recalled:

"We had been on this six-week American tour where we were playing every night, travelling 500 miles a night to the next gig on a bus, and Paul came home from that, exhausted. His older brother was an accountant in the City. So Paul came home and his mother said, 'How was it?' He said, 'I'm tired. I just came in from the airport. I'm exhausted.' Then his brother would come home from work in London and Paul's mother would say, 'Oh, can you go outside and get the coal, Paul? Keith's had a hard day in the city today. He's working, you know.' They never considered what we were doing to be work. And so therefore in the end you get fed up with fighting it, especially if you're not selling records."

What White hints at here is the fact that even during this early stage in the group's recording career they seemed to be waning commercially. However, there was still hope with every new release that they would be able to repeat the success of the debut single. Furthermore, there were other artists in the music business who kept an eye on The Zombies' development.

It is yet another famous tale from The Zombies' catalogue of anecdotes that when visiting Memphis they went up to see Elvis Presley at his house, Graceland. Unfortunately, they found that the king of rock 'n' roll was away filming on that day. However, Presley's father Vernon assured them that his son was very fond of The Zombies and had their records in his private collection.

"I was doing an interview with a guy in Ireland recently," Rod Argent told me. "He asked me about the time we visited Elvis' house in 1965, and I was retelling this story as I have done several times about how Vernon met us at the door and said, 'Oh, Elvis would have loved to have met you guys because he really likes you guys.' I thought that he was just bullshitting. But this Irish guy said, 'Excuse me, I'm a complete Elvis fanatic. Didn't you know that Elvis had your records on his jukebox?' I went, 'Wah!' That just blew me away. The thought that Elvis had completely turned my world around when I was eleven, and that he actually had my songs on his jukebox. That was just like the pinnacle for me."

Sadly, at this stage in his career Presley wasn't personally selecting material for his own records. However, it doesn't take much to imagine him doing a dynamite version of "She's Not There".

14

The good guys don't always win

On returning to the UK in June, The Zombies went to Jackson's Studio to demo early versions of "Whenever You're Ready", "I Know She Will", "I'll Keep Trying" and "You'll Go From Me" (a forerunner of the song "Don't Go Away"). Two of these demos can be found on the *Zombie Heaven* CD box set.

Shortly afterwards, professional recordings of "I'll Keep Trying", "Whenever You're Ready" and "Don't Go Away" were laid down at Decca No. 2.

Sporting a three-part lyric structure, vulnerable lyrics and a dynamic arrangement, "I'll Keep Trying" is another typical Rod Argent song from the borderland between beat group material and the kind of "big songs" that could easily be augmented with a grand arrangement. Sadly, once again the opportunity was missed – for reasons unknown, the mastertape was left on a shelf at Decca until 1968 where it became part of the recordings Chris White refurbished for yet another release that didn't happen (a projected posthumous album titled *Rest In Peace*). A not entirely necessary extra vocal arrangement was added for the occasion and the track was finally released in 1984 on an obscure US compilation LP, *Back Track*. The original, un-overdubbed version can now be found on *Zombie Heaven*.

Rod Argent: "I was amazed at how much I liked that when I heard it on the box set, because I didn't hear it until that came out. Actually, I quite liked the mix on that one. I thought, 'There's one that actually did have something.' However, I very much prefer the unoverdubbed version."

"Whenever You're Ready" is from the same wonderful mould, and at least that was released as a single in September 1965. All the group members expected it would be the hit that would finally break their downwards commercial spiral. Most significantly, the arrangement was built around a riff not terribly different from the one that had propelled "She's Not There" to the top of the charts. But once again, there were problems.

"I think the song again is better than the record," says Colin Blunstone. "It's a lot to do with the harmonies not being as full as they could have been. It just didn't sound as full as it did when we played. I like that song, and I think the record could have been better."

Rod Argent adds, "I remember thinking at the time that 'Whenever You're Ready' could have a real chance. Again, I don't feel the mix was good on it. It was a little bit insubstantial."

When the song eventually came out and flopped, it was a great setback to the band who now started to realise that writing and recording Number 1 hits was a considerably more difficult task than they had first been led to believe.

"It seemed to me that the harder we tried, the more distant

it became," Paul Atkinson said. "We were pretty much all convinced that 'Whenever You're Ready' was going to be a hit. We thought that was going to be the one, and it was a bitter disappointment when it didn't make it. After that I certainly lost a lot of heart, and Colin did too."

Finally from the same day, "Don't Go Away" is another classic Chris White composition, built around sustained bass notes and friendly yet unusual chord changes. The lyrics are best left to his own comment: "God – they are a bit 'lost and lonely', aren't they?"

The main elements and patterns in Argent and White's songwriting have already been pointed out; they would remain in force throughout the group's time with Decca and to a certain extent persist until The Zombies' demise in late 1967. Hence, there is little call for continual analysis, though it is still worth stressing the degree to which the two writers put emphasis on what they themselves describe as "the beauty of melody". A much more difficult feature to define than lyrical content, chord sequences and bass lines, this is probably the strongest quality of their work and one of the main reasons why they continue to win new followers even today, more than thirty years after they folded. Chris White:

"Rod and I did agree that the most important things in songs are the melody and the strong rhythm. You've got to have those to have a popular hit. I'm not saying that's all it should be, but if you want something to be successful... but we didn't always get it right."

On 8 July, after a quick stint in Paris to fulfil a two-night engagement at La Locomotif, the band put down five new tracks for Decca. These were Chris White's "I Love You", "Don't Cry For Me" and "I Know She Will", Rod Argent's "If It Don't Work Out", and finally the second of Colin Blunstone's two compositions for the group, "How We Were Before".

"I Love You" made it on to the B-side of "Whenever You're Ready" and much later (1969) became a hit for a US group called People. Colin Blunstone:

"That was a bit of a heartbreaker. It wasn't a favourite song of mine to be absolutely honest, but it was a little bit disappointing that we were struggling so hard and then later on someone else had a hit with one of Chris' songs."

Surprisingly, White never wrote his songs around bass figures at this time but mainly used acoustic guitar for composing.

"The thing that came first there was the riff," he told me. "That was the root of writing that one. In actual fact I think I nicked that off Tommy Roe!"

Normally, The Zombies would record a number of takes and then simply select the best for adding lead vocal and harmonies. This is very different from the way The Beatles were working around the same time, where final tracks would often consist of bits and pieces from different takes cut together. Apparently, "I Love You" presents a slight exception to this rule:

"I did find out lately that 'I Love You' had an edit at the beginning," White said. "When we recorded it we came straight in with the vocal, and what the producer has done is taken one verse, just as an instrumental track, and copied it onto the beginning. Otherwise, we didn't use edits until later on. We had to get it right when we played it through – it was not like nowadays where they edit everything from the bass drum upwards. It had to be played right because the backing was all on one track."

"Don't Cry For Me" (one of many Zombies songs to include a reference to shedding tears) is an astonishing high-quality pop song with powerful breaks between verses and bridges, driven along by Grundy's excellent drumming and Chris White's increasingly innovative bass-playing. The track sounds at least five years ahead of its time, yet it was another song that ridiculously enough was shelved. It was subsequently among the tracks revived in 1968 where, augmented with extra harmonies, it ended up on the B-side of the highly successful single, "Time Of The Season". To my mind, it could easily have made an A-side in its own right.

In contrast to the energy of "Don't Cry For Me", "I Know She Will" (yet another boy-to-boy conversation) exudes calm and beauty. It is a track which points towards the mood of British rock in the early post-Beatles period. Unfortunately, this is yet another recording which got crudely shelved at the time. Augmented with Mike Vickers' impeccable string arrangement from 1968, it finally emerged on the 2-LP compilation *Time Of The Zombies* in 1973 – at which time the world had finally caught up with it. The entire character of the song and its recording, including Blunstone's clear, pre-pubescent delivery, makes it come across almost as "the big hit Nick Drake never had".

Another song left to gather dust in Decca's vault was the astounding "If It Don't Work Out", an Argent composition with what must be one of the most intriguing vocal lines ever leading from a chorus into a bridge. It was originally written for Dusty Springfield, yet another outstanding performer who, unlike the general public and producer Ken Jones, was aware that something highly interesting and super-innovative was going under the name of The Zombies.

Rod Argent: "We were on tour with Dusty and she said to me, 'Would you write me a song?' So I wrote it over the weekend. She asked me on a Friday, and on Monday I said, 'I've got a song for you.' I wrote it at home, on the piano. She loved it. I can only remember the first day of the recording session Dusty was doing for *Everything's Coming*

Up Dusty [her 1965 LP]. I recorded the piano and I would have loved to have stayed during the whole recording, but for some reason I had to go away. I couldn't stay for the whole thing. But I know she was thinking about that as a single at the time."

The Zombies own version of the song, once again with superb string and vocal arrangements added under the direction of Mike Vickers, was first released as a posthumous US single in 1968 with "Don't Cry For Me" on the flipside.

Finally, there is Colin Blunstone's "How We Were Before", which perhaps doesn't quite measure up to the other material recorded on 6 July but is nevertheless a fine little tune.

"I lived in Hatfield at 27 Cumberland Court in a flat with my parents," he told me. "I think all my early songs are written there. I've never been a very confident songwriter. I'm still not. I sit here playing for hours and hours and just get nowhere."

Blunstone would later continue to write for his own solo career in the seventies and he is still to this day writing first-class songs, but he has never been a prolific artist. Again, there seems to be a lack of self-confidence there which is ironic considering his outstanding talent.

"The others used to pull my leg," he recalls. "There's a bit [in 'How We Were Before'] that goes dum-dum, da-dum. Every time it goes around it ends like that. And they always sang 'God Save The Queen' when that bit came around. I was really a bit precious about this song, and of course they knew that and they pulled my leg."

Rod Argent: "Because I'd happened to write the two big hits I think Colin felt a bit like, 'My God, he's making all that money and I'm not.' We were pretty badly ripped off at that time as far as the 'live' performances were concerned with agencies, etc. We weren't seeing the money as artists that we should have done. But because I'd written those things, and my publishers were very honest, I was actually getting the songwriting royalties. So I think Colin was trying to redress the balance a bit."

A week later, in mid-June 1965, The Zombies embarked on their second major US tour, this time mainly as a double-act with The Searchers.

"It was a lot more relaxed this time," Blunstone recalled. "We also played two or three gigs with the Beach Boys, which I really enjoyed because they were one of my favourite bands. I got a few snaps for my photo collection. In Nashville some gigs got cancelled and we all got stuck there for about five days. So there was a little bit of intermixing."

Colin Blunstone and Chris White in particular were huge Beach Boys fans. Did The Beach Boys in return get turned on to The Zombies' music? We don't know. However, what can be observed is that over the next year Brian Wilson became increasingly innovative on the chord-structure front, incorporating changes of a nature not dissimilar to those in Argent and White's writings, resulting in the *Pet Sounds* LP from 1966. Interestingly, this particular Beach Boys album subsequently became a huge influence on The Zombies second album, *Odessey And Oracle*.

One US group that has always admitted being influenced by The Zombies were the highly successful The Left Banke, who initially got together with the proclaimed sole aim of singing songs from the Argent/White catalogue. The 1966 Left Banke single "Walk Away Renee" became a milestone in popular music, but hundreds of other minor North American acts were strongly influences by The Zombies as well. A typical example is the sadly-underrated Californian cult singer-songwriter Emitt Rhodes and his group at the time, The Merry-Go-Round, who enjoyed a local hit in 1967 with "You're A Very Lovely Women", sporting several Argent/White-influenced chord changes, dramatic dynamics and an orchestral arrangement of the kind The Zombies themselves ironically were never allowed at the time.

Chris White: "In later years we've been very surprised finding out about the people we've influenced. Tom Petty wrote the introduction to the box set, and I was surprised. And I've heard Billy Joel talk about The Zombies. Why is it a surprise? Because we failed, you see. We couldn't sell any records, so to suddenly find yourself mentioned in the same breath as *Sgt. Pepper* and *Pet Sounds* is very strange. But it does give you a feeling of vindication."

Despite their relatively obscure status in their homeland, the group were undoubtedly an influence on some bands there as well. It is already clear that Procol Harum's Matthew Fisher was a devoted fan from early on. Modesty prevents The Zombies themselves from suggesting that they were an inspiration for The Beatles too – I personally think differently. Several Beatles pronounced admiration for The Zombies records right from the beginning. It is obvious that George Harrison was a fan (although he also rightfully pointed out that the group's later records probably wouldn't become chart toppers), and if you look closely you can find several features in Lennon/McCartney compositions from around 1965/66 which suggest at least a subconscious inspiration from The Zombies (a typical example being a surprisingly bluesy chord-change in the otherwise baroque-influenced "For No One" from the *Revolver* LP).

Paul Atkinson: "In fact, when I first met Paul [McCartney] – I worked with him in the seventies – he actually launched into 'She's Not There'. He knew all the words, he sang the whole thing!"

Perhaps statements like these can earn The Zombies the title of "a musicians' band", if that means a band whose qualities are such that other musicians are slightly better equipped to appreciate them.

Amid a schedule of stage appearances and TV shows the group found time to record a new single A-side on 10 November. Titled "Is This The Dream" (and coupled with Blunstone's "How We Were Before") it was yet another track where the band were asked to leave the studio during the mixing, and the tension was running high. Colin Blunstone:

"Ken Jones said, 'Well, okay guys, we're gonna mix it now.' Rod and I went up to the top of the road and had a couple of pints. I thought that song was really, really good. But when I came back and they'd mixed it, I didn't recognise it. I thought that they were in fact playing a very early take or a demo. I don't know what it was, but I didn't recognise it as what we had left behind. Certainly for me the penny was beginning to drop that the producer/band relationship was not as good as it could be. At the next session Rod and Chris wanted to stay for the mix. There was a very big row and they were told very forcibly that they couldn't stay. I was very disappointed with that record."

As with practically all the other Zombies singles, listeners unaware of these debates and minor crises have for decades found much pleasure in "Is This The Dream". I certainly don't think it's a bad slice of 7" vinyl by any means and it is intriguing to wonder what the group themselves really had in mind when they recorded it. However, when I asked Chris White how he would feel about going back to the original master tapes to re-mix some of them along with Rod Argent, he was reluctant, saying that these things were of their time and should not be meddled with afterwards.

15

To write or not to write

Seeing that composing apparently was a much safer source of income than touring, Colin Blunstone wasn't the only member having a stab at being a songwriter. "I did try composing myself," Paul Atkinson told me, "and didn't succeed. Some people have it, and some people don't. I tried really hard, and I did write some things, but they were very, very clichéd and obviously very derivative of distinct songs. I never brought them up to the group. I realised that these are not worthy things to do. They were just experiments on my behalf. It was one of my frustrations, especially when you're surrounded with fresh talent. You want to emulate it. But it's a gift that I don't have."

From early 1966 onwards a split within The Zombies between writing and non-writing members started to show. The fact that by now two group members were pretty well-off, driving around in expensive sports cars, swinging-London style, while the others were struggling to survive or at least convince their parents that this was a viable alternative to getting a steady job or furthering your education, meant that a certain tension started to bounce back and forth between the two factions. Not making any decent money, it seems that Blunstone in particular put pressure on Chris White and Rod Argent to come up with more hit songs. It wasn't an easy task.

"The minute we started to write hit records, or tried to write them, they went wrong," Chris White stated. "You sometimes end up with records that are geared and built for maximum impact. It never sells, and you hated it in the first place, so you've lost everything. All we had to do was keep on writing things we felt inspired us, and then you come up with things. But whenever we tried to write a hit record, it never worked. Everyone thinks people have a formula, but the only one who had a formula was Phil Spector, and that was a sound formula.

"We'd sit down and analyse: what's the common denominator? We got the bass line here doing that, interesting rhythm and a riff pattern. But the funny thing is if you create it like that you come up with crap. Something happens; it's very difficult to explain. If you do it from the heart, and not from the head, it's much better for some reason. You can then say, 'Ah, you could apply that formula-thing there,' and you build upon the original idea. But if you build the formula first and try to add to it, it's bound to go wrong."

Rod Argent: "It was just a bit of a forced atmosphere, and we weren't in control of the proceedings. That was the problem. I'm not saying we should have had control over every aspect. We shouldn't have had that, we didn't know enough. But we weren't enough in control of our own performances. The first album wasn't done without respect at all, but from Ken's point of view it was very much an attitude of, 'Well, we've got to cash in on the single.' In some ways he respected us a lot, and he respected the music and the talent, but it was just a little bit of an old fashioned attitude about some of the things.

"We didn't panic. But if Ken had gone in there and thought, 'Actually, the thing that made 'She's Not There' a hit was that we took whatever the group had and made the best of it.' Rather than thinking that what made the song a hit was Colin's breathiness and we're going to emphasise that. Instead, if he'd just said, 'What we will try to do is emphasise the talent of the group on the first record and bring out whatever was there, make the best of whatever they presented on the night, and we'll apply that to the rest of the sessions,' I think we would have turned out some more hits."

According to Chris White, there were several more factors explaining why the group had lost their initial momentum:

"I think probably part of the problem in England was that we didn't have a 'guitar hero', and that two of us wore glasses. Plus the fact that the keyboard is an instrument you're sitting down with. There are also sexual things as well, like a sax player can be sexy, and a lead guitarist can as well. But a lead guitarist can be sexy to the men as well as the women, because they'll all play air guitar. It's power, and it's so visual – the keyboard player isn't."

I asked Rod Argent if he never felt Paul Atkinson ought to have been a bit more outgoing as a guitarist.

"Not necessarily," he replied. "Paul never had that sort of Clapton or Hendrix sound. That wasn't his style. And I guess one of the things that was unusual about us was that we were a group that were more dominated by keyboards than guitar. But there's a million guitar groups out there."

Atkinson himself, I found, is no stranger to the argument:

"I was the only guitarist in the group, so on stage I was used to this role of playing a combination of rhythm and lead guitar, especially on some of the early R&B covers we used to do. But the songs that Rod was writing weren't written for lead guitar. They were written for 'lead piano'. I couldn't compete on a musical level with Rod. He was a far better musician than I will ever be. It was obvious right from the start that Rod was the best musician in the group and he was the leader of the group, without question. The kind of songs that Rod had written mostly featured the keyboards. There were exceptions like 'Tell Her No', which was definitely featuring a guitar intro, but the songs he wrote didn't really lend themselves to blazing guitar solos. It wasn't that kind of music. I wasn't too unhappy with it. I didn't fancy myself as a blazing lead guitarist, a Clapton or a Beck. I wasn't that kind of a player. So I was kind of content with that role of providing the rhythm guitar and the occasional guitar figure, which I played frequently by playing harmony with the keyboard. Clearly, the distinctive instrument in the group was keyboards."

Anyone questioning this statement should take a listen to an LP of US bands doing Zombies tributes, recorded in the early nineties and released under the title "World Of The Zombies" (not to be confused with the Decca Zombies compilation-LP of the same name). The groups featured here present songs from the Argent/White catalogue in considerably more guitar-heavy arrangements than the originals, and the result is – I'm sorry to say – not particularly convincing, at least not to this writer's ears (getting the chords wrong in several cases doesn't help).

In truth, Paul Atkinson is a very capable guitarist, but he suffers the fate of rhythm players in general in that his contributions can be difficult to detect. Their job is more to contribute to the overall feel of the music. Ironically, to really "hear" them you'd have to cut them out! Such a thing, of course, isn't normally possible and neither is the alternative of omitting other instruments or voices in the mix to make the rhythm guitar come more to the fore. However, courtesy of Chris White I have listened to all the original takes made of "She's Not There" during the group's first session for Decca, without vocal overdubs, and believe me the guitarist *is* steady. He is also delicate and tasteful in his playing, a fine musician indeed and superbly suited to the group's entire style.

Chris White, I'm sure, agrees with this and his pointing at Atkinson's lack of aggression in his playing as an explanation for the band's difficulties in maintaining their commercial success is purely a statement of fact, not an artistic criticism. This is also the case when it comes to White's description of Colin Blunstone's position in the band:

"Colin was never totally happy on stage. He wasn't a natural stage person. He wasn't Mick Jagger or John Lennon or McCartney. I mean, he was okay, because he had this fantastic voice. There is no other like it. But every time we were out he would ask people, 'What's your job? Oh, you're a photographer, that's a good one, I might be interested in that.' And when The Zombies finished he couldn't wait to get back into insurance, so he could stop worrying about things."

"Maybe Colin was a bit of a worrier," Hugh Grundy agreed. "Perhaps he didn't think he was cutting it as well as he would have liked. Dissatisfied in his own abilities. I don't think, and I wouldn't for one minute mean this disparagingly to him, but he's not the extrovert that a stage performer needs to be. Having said that I'll qualify that instantly by adding that in the last few years I would dispute my own argument. I've seen him on stage several times now, and his voice just continues to improve. But even in the old days he used to jump about, he used to enjoy himself, no doubt about that. Perhaps in the studio he didn't jump about quite so much.

But I don't mean that as any criticism. We always worked hard in the studio. We always thoroughly enjoyed it, certainly I did. He didn't see himself as a lead singer from the start, and now and again he used to say to Rod, 'No, you sing it, you sing that. You're better than me.' Rod had the devil's own job persuading him, 'No, you're the one with the voice, you sing it.' Fortunately he did, and fortunately one or two of those songs were hits. Maybe Rod just picked on the fact that Colin's voice was unique. And that's where it stands. Voices that are unique get on."

Blunstone himself pointed to another problem:

"I had the feeling that what we were involved with was a passing fad," he said. "For instance, when we were on the road in the early days, Rod and I were walking around the town we were going to play in, and I said to him, 'Oh Rod, if we all come out of this with £500 and we can keep it going for six months or a year I think it wouldn't have been too bad.' And I could see that he was really angry with me, because he knew right from the beginning that he wanted to be in the music business. That was what he wanted to do, but I didn't know. To me it was just something that had happened to us and I was really enjoying it, but I didn't think it would last very long."

Paul Atkinson: "I guess we were really trying to achieve commercial success. We were trying to get a hit single again. Maybe too desperate, in retrospect. Perhaps we were trying too hard. Because it was a singles world you really had no career unless you had a hit single. So we were getting a bit testy with each other. I don't remember anyone threatening to walk out, but Colin was pretty vocal about how unhappy he was. I was too, but less vocal. I think it really hurt Colin a lot, as the lead singer of the group, to feel that he was really not making a living. That was the toughest thing, to put all this effort into it and then not see a reasonable reward. I felt the same way, but Colin was far more visible and, let's be honest, his voice was the group and so I think he had more of a beef."

The bleakness of the situation in the Zombies camp is underlined by the fact that during the whole of 1966, the band recorded only five tracks for their label. Of these, four were laid down sometime in May or June at Landsdowne Studios and comprised "Indication", "I'll Call You Mine," "She Does Everything For Me" and a cover, "Gotta Get A Hold Of Myself".

"We changed studio from Decca to Landsdowne," Rod Argent told me. "We just wanted to ring some changes, really. We felt that the records could sound more ballsy than they did. We felt that was down to Ken, but we said to Ken, 'We really feel that the records could sound a bit more substantial.' His response to that was, 'Why don't we try Landsdowne Studios?'"

For people unaware of the story behind the Argent-composed "Indication", it sounds like a great, classic psychedelic single A-side, a pure, harmony-laden sixties pop song with a long, apparently Arabian-influenced (*sic*) chant at the end. However, the arrangement came about in a rather peculiar manner.

Rod Argent: "We used to do a Jimmy Reed song on stage, a blues thing called 'Baby What You Want Me To Do'. At the end of that I used to go into this long improvisation based around 'God Rest You Merry Gentlemen'! It was quite bizarre. I even used to start singing along with the improvisation. It got quite wild. We wanted to use that on a record. So that's what we did on "Indication", with a guitar sound that was supposed to be really out in the background. It was supposed to be this thing we used to do on stage and which went down a storm. But when Ken mixed it he didn't think that was commercial, so he just put the guitar up really loud.

Consequently, the record does not sound as it was conceived. That was another thing we were really annoyed about."

Today, however, Rod Argent has had to change his perception of Ken Jones' input: "When I went back and heard that again I was pleasantly surprised," he told me. "In fact, when I'm doing 'Indication' with Colin on stage now, we do it like the record!"

If "Indication" had an overall optimistic feel to its lyric, so did Chris White's "I'll Call You Mine". Once again, this was an excellent Zombies track which Decca decided to forget about until two years later, when the success of "Time Of The Season" meant that there was suddenly a new demand for releases by the group.

"This session was the first time we used double-tracking for harmonies," said Chris White. "But that was also one of the first reasons we started pushing for us to produce ourselves. We still weren't allowed to be in on the mixes, which started getting a bit wishy-washy. It wasn't coming out like we were playing it 'live' even."

"She Does Everything For Me" was another new Argent composition which managed to be energetic, melodic and musically adventurous all at the same time but was poorly treated by Decca, who apparently didn't find it had potential to be a single A-side.

"I thought at the time it sounded pretty good," Rod Argent said, "and I really enjoy listening to it now. We double-tracked the voices, and we were knocked out by what seemed to us at the time to be a pretty massive sound."

The final track from the session was yet another sign that things where getting shaky within the group. Rod Argent:

"We did that because people were saying at that time – Tito Burns in particular – 'You don't have to do your own songs all the time. You stand much more of a chance of getting a hit if you do somebody else's songs.'"

The Zombies had first heard "Gotta Get A Hold Of Myself" – formerly a single for Little Anthony And The Imperials – on the Dick Clark Tour and had subsequently incorporated it into their stage repertoire. However, their own recording of it wasn't particularly impressive. In fact, the entire idea of recording other people's compositions seems ludicrous in the view of all the classic Argent and – particularly – White compositions which for more than a year had been habitually recorded and then quietly filed away by Decca. Even Colin Blunstone, one of the spokesmen for trying out cover material on records, now agrees that it was a bad plan:

"Although I had been saying maybe we should do outside songs, I didn't particularly like it to be honest. I remember we did it on a TV show for America. Gracious me! It was a variety programme and they had circus acts and dancing girls. I was put about 30 feet away from the rest of the band with elephants and dancing girls going in between us, and this song is a very close-harmony song that Rod and I sang – I couldn't hear myself, I couldn't hear him. When this TV show came on in the UK I felt so depressed. I remember I drove down to one of the local pubs. I thought, 'I'm just going to have a couple of beers and calm down.' It could have been any pub in the area, but I'd only been there two seconds when Rod walked in and said, 'My God, did you just see that!' But we were all very relieved because in America, in the middle of the show, President Johnson made a speech to the nation and, thank God, his speech covered our spot. We were quite pleased with that. Sometimes when people put these shows on and they want you to play 'live' they don't realise you've got to be able to hear one another. Otherwise it's just going all over the place. That wasn't one of our finest moments."

On the whole, 1966 wasn't the most uplifting point in

The Zombies' career. In October, they recorded their final track for Decca at Kingsway Studios. Initially built around the requirements of legendary producer-madman Joe Meek, Kingsway was an all-round musical environment, technically flawless but not particularly suited to rock groups. Furthermore, things went somewhat wrong for Ken Jones in the recording process. To make space for an overdubbed horn section the producer chose to record the lead vocal on the same track as some of the instrumentation. It was subsequently found that the vocal wasn't loud enough, but since nothing could be done to rectify this a new vocal had to be dubbed on to the existing recording, making for a pretty strange final sound. Were it not for the inclusion of "She Does Everything For Me" on the flip, this record would be best forgotten.

"The cracks were starting to appear during that year," Paul Atkinson told me. "There were brief flashes of success, like the visit to Paris, and then the last one I guess was the Philippines. Although we were ripped off, it was a success. We sold out ten days at this huge colosseum. In the UK we were playing colleges and occasional small clubs. None of us had any appetite to continue with that. There was no future in it."

16

Machine guns and meditation

The trip to The Philippines during March 1967 has become one of the big stories in the legend of The Zombies, calling for the band to retell their experiences endlessly with much smiling and irony. However, at the time it doesn't seem to have been much fun. Colin Blunstone told me how the idea for the journey came about in the first place:

"By this time we still had the same manager. He would be sending contracts to me. I remember thinking, 'Oh, this sounds quite good.'"

It did indeed. The Philippines was an exotic place, the group would be paid £75 a night, plus free accommodation and meals. All in all, it seemed like a summer holiday with everything paid for and a salary on top. The band's assumption was that they would be playing the occasional gig in the foyer of a hotel.

However, what they didn't realise was that they had some four or five records in the Philippine Top Ten and were immensely popular there. They arrived at three o'clock in the morning, yet to their complete surprise found the airport packed with fans yelling and screaming and generally going crazy. All the way to the hotel their car was surrounded by fans on bicycles, on motorcycles and in cars. "I thought someone was going to get killed," Blunstone told me.

He continues: "We got to the Areneta Stadium, which holds over 30,000 people. The first show I think we played to 28,000 on a Friday night. Then we played a matinée to 15,000, and then Saturday night it was about 32,000 people. All in all we played for ten nights, and we were getting £75 a night! That was for the whole band. We said, 'We'd like to stay on but we want proper money.' The promoter over there was a very, very tough nut, a multi-millionaire guy who owned this stadium. He had his own militia there with guns. He said, 'Listen. If you stay here, you work for me and you work for the money I'm prepared to give you.'"

Not very pleased with this proposition, the group flew to Hong Kong where they got in touch with "a Chinese businessman over there we used to call S.Y." He owned the record company which released The Zombies' records in the Philippines and helped arrange for them to get some further dates there.

However, when they arrived the local promoter – seeing that they were now working for someone else – tried to get them thrown in prison.

"As you know, it's quite a scary place," said Blunstone. "Well, it just went on from there. Because we'd come back and we weren't working for him he tried to get rival radio stations to say that we weren't coming. So there was a lot of confusion over whether we were going to play or not."

One of the gigs the group were supposed to perform was

in a large nightclub in Manilla called the Nile Club. They set their gear up, did the sound-check and were just about to go on stage when the owners suddenly changed their mind and wouldn't let them play. They had received certain threats.

Instead the group went on to another club where they were allowed to play. However the following morning, sitting on an plane and reading the papers, they discovered that the club they had just played had been burned down during the night. Colin Blunstone:

"We found out, that is for a fact, when we were playing the Philippines, and we were getting £75 per night between us of which Tito took 20%, and we were playing to 30,000 a night – one of his staff admitted that there were two sets of contracts. He said to the man there, 'I'll give you The Zombies for £1,000 if you just say £75.' And he took 20% of our £75!"

Arriving back from the Philippines, The Zombies found themselves at the lowest point ever in their career. Their relationship with Ken Jones had clearly run its course, and without any pronounced animosity the band and their producer parted ways. This also meant that the band's association with Decca had come to and end. All in all it was a "nothing left to lose" situation, which luckily proved to be exactly the creative push the group needed.

Paul Atkinson: "We had the idea, 'What the hell, we're gonna make some music to please ourselves before we break up.' It was kind of sad but at the same time it was a relief, because we didn't have to think, 'Well, this song has to be a hit single.' We just went in and made an album, which was quite a novel thing for a band to do in those days. We did it as a last, defiant gesture. We still wanted to have a hit, but we weren't sacrificing everything to get one."

Around The Zombies the world was changing fast. So fast, in fact, that the Britain they returned to in late March

1967 was probably considerably different to the Britain they had left at the end of the previous month. In pop music particularly, trends were shifting very fast. Within youth culture, drugs were becoming increasingly influential along with growing political, religious and sexual awareness.

How did five young men from suburban St Albans, who were brought up in the environment of a semi-elitist Victorian education, and whose parents were working for what to some extent was a British weapons manufacturer, react to all this? Did they turn into "psychedelic gods", as they were hailed some thirty years later by a music critic?

The answer to such a question must depend on the interpretation of the term. If "psychedelic" means influenced artistically by the use of chemical substances such as LSD, the members of The Zombies completely disavow the term.

Chris White: "None of us took any drugs. We just got drunk instead. The other thing didn't appeal. There wasn't any need. None. Nothing. I didn't do any cannabis at all until the mid-seventies, because I didn't smoke. In fact, Hugh was the only one in The Zombies who smoked cigarettes. Later on, we'd seen far too many casualties of LSD to even dream of taking it. It just didn't appeal to put chemicals into your system."

Colin Blunstone: "I didn't see any drugs, let alone take part in any. I don't think from '64 until '67 there was that much in the way of drugs, to be honest. Later on there was. There must have been pills around, but I didn't see any. I didn't even see anyone smoking a funny cigarette up until '67. Later on there was a lot of things around, but not during that time. It might have been around, but I didn't see it. I'd tell you if I did."

Rod Argent confirmed these views: "In my whole life I think I took a couple of Purple Hearts [amphetamine tablets] when I was in Germany once. But I've always felt it's up to people to do whatever they want. I wasn't trying to tell people not to smoke or do acid, it was just something I didn't want to do. Later on, I certainly did tell my children not to do drugs, but I'm sure they've experimented. For all the talk of the drug culture starting in the sixties, around the time when we started, in the early to mid-sixties, there were very little drugs. They really weren't around. You could find them if you *really* wanted to, but they weren't everywhere. It was only in the late sixties that acid started to become very available. Then it changed a lot. But in '64-'65 it was generally not a drug culture. Not even in the States, as far as I came across. In the seventies when Argent were playing, you'd go into the Fillmore or something and do a gig and the smell of dope was just completely overwhelming. But in the sixties, no. People used to get drunk, but that was it, generally speaking."

This issue of drinking, rather than taking drugs, came back frequently during my interviews with all ex-Zombies.

"We certainly weren't non-drinkers," Hugh Grundy emphasised. "I don't think a great deal was made of it, but I can remember going on stage once or twice and be totally the worse for wear. It was very unprofessional, if you like, but we did it once or twice I have to say."

It also appears that with regard to sexual experiences the group weren't quite the bunch of choir boys that the press continually made them out to be.

"It was not as blatant and rampant as you see it these days," Grundy continued. "In those days we were much more restricted. It wasn't talked about so much, but of course we had girlfriends and we did everything and maybe more than is done these days. Once we started doing universities and touring the world, and maybe the Philippines and places like that – it was a bit of an eye-opener for me, if you like. It made me grow up quick. I remember playing universities and meeting our chums that we'd gone to school with and thinking how naïve they were. I talked to them and they'd tell us stories about what they'd been up to and I thought, 'Oh my God, we've seen ten times worse than that or done this or done that,' and so and so.

Religious philosophy, often Eastern-inspired, is another phenomenon often mentioned in connection with youth cultures during the later part of the sixties and at least two of the band members, Chris White and Rod Argent, had a stint with meditation founded in Buddhism.

"I suppose I was nominally Church of England," White told me. "I tried the Baptist, the Methodist, the Congregationalists and all that sort of thing, I was interested in religion, but I suppose I'm more of a Buddhist now, a Spiritualist, I mean – I do believe in Spiritualism. I've had so many special experiences, but I can't convert anybody."

Rod Argent: "Religion has always played a part in my life, but not in an organised way. I have a view of what I think God is, which is basically the intelligence behind the Universe or the order, or what the Universe is to me. I've always been interested in that side of things, perhaps because of being in the choir, but I've never felt that I subscribed very strongly to anything particularly organised. However, I've always felt praying was powerful, and I still do."

Turned on by The Beatles' interest in Eastern mysticism, Argent and White decided that they wanted a taste of this philosophy themselves and started attending meditation classes.

"We went along to this centre," Argent recalled. "At that time they were suggesting a donation, they didn't say, 'You should give...' whatever it was of your income. I only ever saw it as a technique, and I found it very useful. I used to use it as a technique for relaxation and focusing. It worked very well for me. I never saw anything more deeply religious in that. I occasionally use it now if I need to calm down or whatever. I found it transcendent to some degree, but all this business of yogis flying and things, I never subscribed to anything like that. They just gave you the mantra and you went back a couple of times. They just checked on how it was all going and that was all I ever got into it for, really. It wasn't a substitute for taking LSD or anything. The idea of taking LSD to me, personally, always seemed like a very crude way of messing with the brain. It didn't seem to me to be any way to obtain any sort of revelation. It just seemed to be a way of causing effects in the brain by short-circuiting it. I just seemed very crude, and that's why I didn't do it. Also it sounded very dangerous. It was like if you got a sophisti-cated computer and throw a spanner into the middle of its electronics you're going to get an effect. It felt a little bit like messing with the miracle of the wiring of the brain. So meditation was not a substitute for that. It was just some-thing very interesting, and when I tried it I liked some of the effects it had and from time to time I've used it."

Chris White somewhat contradicts this: "Rod and I both studied meditation in '66 or thereabouts. We did medita-tion regularly. So therefore we had that sudden sweep of vision. The ecstasy stage you can achieve in meditation is better than a drug high, and that might have saved us from getting into drugs. Some of the experiences under medita-tion will give you all sorts of visions and joy."

There are obviously direct influences from meditation in the change of direction apparent in the two songwriters' production from late 1966 onwards. In would also seem that these are songs written by two people with quite simi-lar kinds of traumas caused by failed relationships. Argent's haunting "A Love That Never Was" (based on a chord sequence reminiscent of The Seeds' "Can't Seem To Make You Mine") appears to be lyrically very directly inspired by the kinds of images you can experience during meditation, while Chris White's "I Don't Want To Worry" almost comes across as a mantra.

Another song of White's from the same transitional period, "One Day I'll Say Goodbye", sounds to me a less-successful repetition of the theme in "I Must Move", but "Out Of The Day" is a highly unusual and interesting song, full of flashing images and rhythmic changes. Equally impressive is "Call Of The Night", a forerunner for the lyrically considerably less challenging "Girl Help Me", recorded later by an early incarnation of the group Argent and erroneously released as a Zombies track – yet another song hinting at the melancholy that would also grace Nick Drake's albums a few years down the line.

In their original form none of these songs managed to get past the demo stage, and even as demos none of them saw the light of day until the release of the 1997 *Zombie Heaven* box set. From an outside point of view, they seem to indicate serious upheavals in the lives of Chris White and Rod Argent. Again, it must be mentioned that they both strongly deny any such personal connections and insist on completely detaching the subject matter in their songs from their private lives.

"There was a woman who used to write for *Disc* magazine called Penny Valentine," Rod Argent recalls. "She used to love our stuff and she always used to say, 'How can someone so young have experienced so much heartbreak.' And I thought, 'I haven't experienced any heartbreak!'"

Nevertheless, for Rod Argent the Decca period rounds itself off in an almost uncanny manner, at least on the lyrical front. It all started with the morbid trauma of "She's Not There" and then moved through all the phases of trying to overcome the heartache, ending with the optimism of finding a new loved one as featured in "She Does Everything For

Me". After an intermediate phase of recovery and realisation – "A Love That Never Was" – the stage is set for an entirely new phase with an abundance of new inspirations.

"I wouldn't put the shift in style down to meditation," Rod Argent said, "but the whole business of the *Odessey And Oracle* album felt like a real change."

All in all, by the summer of 1967 the group was standing at a very important crossroads. They would have either to break up now, or to make one last attempt in the recording studio. In this all-or-nothing situation they chose to follow their own instincts entirely, become their own producers and make the kind of music they felt most strongly about without any attempts to be commercial.

Ironically, it was in these circumstances they came up with their second Number 1 single, and also what is now generally reckoned to be one of the very best albums ever made by a rock group.

17

Changes

The spring and summer of 1967 proved to be an exceedingly creative period for songwriters Chris White and Rod Argent.

"We actually felt that energy from the 'Summer of Love'," Chris White told me. "A lot of people used to just get a 'high', but the sweep was a definite feeling, be it right or wrong. It was rather akin to the national feeling when Princess Diana died. You could feel it in the air. Now, whether that was morose or undeserved or whatever doesn't matter, it was a mass-emotion. I had never seen anything like it. It wasn't Messianic, more like crowd hysteria. I actually think that if you think badly of somebody, they actually do feel it. It's a physical thing. And if you feel good about somebody, then it's the same thing. So if everybody's feeling the same thing, it gathers its own momentum. It becomes a giant thing, and nobody's immune to it.

"I'm sure any movement has people jumping on the band-wagon, but all I can say is that we genuinely felt it ourselves. We felt the enlightenment, not being religious or anything like that, but the sudden realisation of a different conscious-stage."

In some interviews Rod Argent has pronounced feelings towards the hippie movement like those expressed above by Chris White. However, during my interviews I found him somewhat less enthusiastic:

"At the time I just felt it was all a bit naïve. I wasn't against it. I would have loved the world to suddenly put down all its violence, but I just didn't think that sitting around smoking and saying, 'Oh, everything's cool, man,' was really the way to any sort of real sense of peace."

Perhaps the one record which above all signified the summer of 1967 was Procol Harum's "A Whiter Shade Of Pale".

"I went to a party with Rod when that first came out," Colin Blunstone recalled. "It went on all night this party, and we played 'A Whiter Shade Of Pale' all night! It was only a little record player, so we put it on 'repeat'. I just absolutely loved it. It may have had an influence on *Odessey And Oracle*."

Rod Argent also recalled the occasion and added: "I imme-diately went out and bought it. I remember thinking at the time, 'My God, a Hammond organ with a slow Leslie [*see Glossary*] is something which I'd thought for ages we should do something with, because it sounds so great. And now someone's bloody well got there ahead of me!'

"The thing that struck me with 'A Whiter Shade Of Pale' was the sort of quasi-Bach thing, which I thought was very cool. I didn't think about the bass line just descending."

However, the art of the descending bassline was already well-incorporated into The Zombies' idiom, and in fact during the mid-sixties there was a whole handful of hits utilising this technique, such as Percy Sledge's "When A Man Loves A Woman", The Beatles' "For No One", The Moody Blues' "Go Now". Chris White and Rod Argent don't recall their composing and arranging techniques changing directly because of the release of these records, but it is nevertheless a fact that several songs on *Odessey And Oracle* feature the phenomenon of descending basslines taken to a new extreme, and also the introduction of the Hammond organ, taking the place of Argent's beloved Hohner Pianette and the occasional Vox organ. To put it another way – I find it very difficult to imagine songs like "Care Of Cell 44" and, particularly, "Beechwood Park" being written and arranged before the release of the Procol Harum single (though it must be said that the time-frame only just allows for an inspiration to have taken place).

Even more strikingly *Odessey And Oracle* reminds me of The Beach Boys' ground-breaking album *Pet Sounds*, released during the previous year. Surprisingly Rod Argent, though he remembers liking this album, doesn't recall being particularly inspired by it:

"I always liked the Beach Boys, but I never took them on board as such. I would never say that the Beach Boys were an influence."

However, with Chris White it is a different matter: "*Pet Sounds* was a shock to me. I got goosebumps just thinking about it. A genius piece of work. I think there is a lot of Beach Boys in *Odessey And Oracle*. I think we wanted to make an album after hearing *Pet Sounds* and what The Beatles had done, creating an entity, a whole thing. We were so pleased, we enjoyed it when we did *Odessey And Oracle*, it just came together. And very little studio time was used up."

In fact the band's entire budget for recording the album appears to have been a meagre £1,000.

"I read an interview with Peter Vince," White continued, "who used to record us at Abbey Road. He said, 'In actual fact, they were the first non-EMI group to record there.' And we didn't know that. But our sessions were still very short."

Rod Argent: "Chris and I suddenly had the freedom to experiment in whatever way we wanted to, even though by modern-day standards we still did things very quickly. It just felt like a very freeing thing and it led to a difference in the way we approached the recording sessions and the way we approached the writing. It was to do with being liberated from the old regime, I think." Whatever the case may be, during a few months in the spring and summer of 1967 Rod Argent and Chris White either wrote from scratch or polished up a set of highly accomplished tunes, which they then presented to the band at rehearsals in a small church hall in Wheathampstead near St Albans.

As always before, a considerable part of the arranging was done by the entire group.

"In other groups often the songwriter was the man and that was it," Hugh Grundy stated. "And when Rod or Chris had written a new song they'd play it to us and say, 'We'd like you to do this on it.' But after that it was very much a situation where we'd all suggest things. Neither of them were in any way dogmatic about the way they wanted their songs done. I think that was the success, and that is the reason that we are still friends even today. You look at a lot of groups, they get very big-headed about it, egos take over and then hatred sets in which can last for the rest of your lives. But with us, we're all still friends."

This ability to stay friends also seems to have distinguished the group in other relationships as well. As already mentioned, the break between them and producers Ken Jones and Joe Roncoroni was amicably solved with an agreement that the partnership had run its course and it was time for all parties to try something new.

Following that, Argent and White had started approaching labels with a view to recording The Zombies' second LP and producing it themselves. CBS went for the idea, a deal was signed, and the recordings at Abbey Road started on 1 June. Since the next chapter will contain a major critique of the entire album, we shall concentrate here mainly on the individual band members' own recollections of the events.

On 1 June the band put down the backing tracks for two songs, Chris White's "Friends Of Mine" and Argent's "A Rose For Emily". Right from the beginning there was a feeling that something new and positive was on its way. So spirits were high, though there was also a serious time pressure. Chris White:

"When we went to Abbey Road people like Geoff Emerick and Peter Vince engineered us. They had been doing all the Beatles stuff and we could get great drum sounds. We really enjoyed that recording, but it was very few sessions. We did it in bits and pieces, because we only had this £1,000 budget. So we'd record three songs after we'd written and rehearsed them. We were very strong on rehearsals before getting in the studios. And we'd sometimes do three songs in two three-hour sessions."

White continued to relate to me his feelings about the new song of his that was recorded during this very first session at Abbey Road:

"I still like it though it was a bit twee... It was originally very slow and we thought, 'No, let's do it faster.' It took me a very short time to write it, but when we came to rehearse it we said, 'Why don't we do a chant underneath it?' So we used different names of people – of which only one couple has remained married, one person is dead, most of them are divorced. That's trying to be positive in a song, as opposed to losing everything."

About the other song recorded on the same day, "A Rose For Emily", Rod Argent recalls: "I got the idea for it, although it didn't bear any relation to it, from a William Faulkner short story. It's got nothing to do with what's in Faulkner's story, that was just where I got the idea for the title from. It was one of those mornings where I got up, I'd just read the short story, and I really liked the title. So I started messing around at the piano. Suddenly a song was there. It was just like that, really. It was just me enjoying working at the piano with this image in my mind. Lyrically I suppose it is an elaboration of the theme on The Beatles' 'Eleanor Rigby'. It has to do with loneliness. We tried it with a cello part, but in the end I preferred it simpler."

The cello version is now available on the *Zombie Heaven* box set, though it seems to add little to the band's story apart from confirming what Argent states here – it was better without it.

"A Rose For Emily" was different from the majority of previous Zombies recordings for not having a rhythm section, just piano and vocals. There are several similar arrangements on *Odessey And Oracle*, so I asked Hugh Grundy if he felt somewhat left out during the recording of the album.

"That wasn't a problem," he replied. "That was what they fancied doing and I think some of those tracks were lovely. It doesn't matter that I wasn't on it at all. It's still Zombies and it's still us. I'm sure I was there chipping in the odd comment like, 'Can't you do this, why don't you try that?'"

The group returned on the following day and laid down the backing for another surprisingly light-hearted Chris White composition titled "This Will Be Our Year". One of the most immediately striking features on this recording is the significant technical development White's bass playing had undergone during the previous year. He had now changed from his short-necked Gibson bass to a Fender Precision.

"When the box set came out, Rod phoned me up," White told me. "He said, 'I know it's a bit late, but there's some fantastic bass playing on there. I know it's 30 years too late, but I'm really impressed!'

After more than a month's break the group resumed working on their new album on 10 and 11 July, recording the Argent-penned "Hung Up On A Dream", perhaps the song on the album that, more than any other, has prompted the band to be labelled psychedelic. Again, Chris White seems more positive in his statements about the hippie phenomenon than Rod Argent, who wrote the song.

"It's funny when you hear 'Hung Up On A Dream', we really felt it," White stated. "There was that sudden movement at that time of the 'Love Generation'."

I asked White if he found it possible to detach these feelings, which he appears to have strongly subscribed to, from the drug culture, which he feels just as strongly was "not for me".

"It's a debatable point," he says. "I think what some people have heard as drug references on *Odessey And Oracle* is more like an epiphany of religious hallucination rather than a drug-induced one. I read an article once about some Zen Buddhists taking LSD and saying, 'Well, that's exactly like a meaningful walk.' They saw a similarity between this drug-taking and Eastern philosophy, which was a discipline in meditation."

Rod Argent picks up the story: "When the box set came out, that was a song I hadn't heard for years and years. I was dreading hearing it again, because though I actually hated all the Haight Ashbury things and that 'Summer of Love' and everything, all the hippie thing, it just impinged on the consciousness enough to infiltrate the lyrics on this one song. So when the compilation came out I spun it and gave it a listen, and I actually thought it sounded great. Again I just looked at the lyrics as a little bit of a period piece, and within that context I thought it was fine."

The recording is also significant for featuring an up-front guitar solo on a Zombies record. It is a rehearsed, classically-inspired piece inserted into the song, pointing towards a future where progressive rock groups such as Genesis would work with similar arrangements.

"To me it was also a pointer of where The Zombies *could* have gone," Paul Atkinson told me, obviously regretful that the band broke up later that same year. This seems para-doxical compared with occasional statements made by Rod Argent that the disbanding was mainly caused by the con-tinuing decline in enthusiasm among the non-songwriting members of the group. It's difficult not to conclude that on this point there was a lack of communication between the two factions. Paul Atkinson:

"I've heard interviews with some of the other guys, and I think Rod said that I was getting sidetracked or distracted with other interests. I don't remember that. I used to love those sessions. I loved these songs, I loved playing them. That was a fantastic summer. We had these wonderful songs, we rehearsed them all very, very carefully and we went into Abbey Road to record. I had a great time. My memory of that is actually the best memory of any of our recording ses-sions.

"There was some friction, but I don't remember it entailing me. I think it entailed more Colin and Rod. The only thing that was distracting me at the time, quite frankly, was my fiancée Molly. We were going through some difficulties. In fact we ended up getting married that October, but during the summer of '67 we were having a lot of difficulties at the same time as the recording was going on. That may have been a distraction, but there were certainly no musical distractions for me.

"The other thing that bothered me and Colin was, frankly, money. We were broke. We weren't supporting ourselves. That was less of an issue for Rod and Chris because of their songwriting income. But I was going to be a married man soon and I was wondering how to make a living. But the music and the sessions were fabulous. I really loved doing that."

20 July saw the recording of a highly unusual song, Chris White's "Butcher's Tale", based on strong feelings over what private soldiers had to go through during the First World War. The arrangement features mainly a harmonium and White making his first ever appearance as lead vocalist.

"I was living in a flat then," he told me. "In a junk shop I found an old pump organ. It was covered in woodworm and the bellows needed replacing, but it was a great thing to play. I was very into the First World War, and I thought, 'If The Bee Gees can write about the 1941 New York mining disaster...' because I thought that was great. I thought, 'Let's do something other than love songs, but just as miserable!' Actually, I wrote that one for Colin, but my shaky little voice worked very well on it because it sounded part of the thing.

"A lot of young men in the First World War were shamed into enlisting. They didn't know what was going on. If they'd known perhaps they wouldn't have been so eager. Possibly their minds couldn't conceive the idiots that ran things. I remember reading about it, and I was driving in my car and all of a sudden the enormity of '60,000 men dying before breakfast', and how many people it would affect, especially since they were coming from the same areas, so whole streets of men would be wiped out – all that just hit me right there.

I saw red and I had to pull over the car. It was almost like a sort of palpitation. Suddenly it hit me how big it was – the horror of the loss."

The track also features some frightening sound effects:

"There were no synthesizers in those days," White continued, "so I had a piece of *Musique Concrète*, which I liked. We reversed the tape, slowed it down, added breathing on to it, and the thing at the end is just an oscillator which Rod played on another track."

Again, there was no percussion on the recording. Nevertheless, Hugh Grundy clearly recalls the occasion and, particularly, the huge harmonium Chris White had brought along on that day.

"I can remember carrying in the bloody thing," Grundy mused. "That's my contribution as much as anything!"

Sometime during July and August (the dating becomes uncertain here) three tracks were recorded, White's "Maybe After He's Gone" and "Beechwood Park", along with Rod Argent's "I Want Her She Wants Me".

"'Maybe After He's Gone' was written on the piano at home," Chris White recalled. "I always liked that tension between the bass notes and the chords. I use it too much, actually! It's such an easy thing to give an atmosphere. I did 'Beechwood Park' on a piano as well. I loved the way that turned out. In the village where my parents used to live, Markyate, there was a private girls' school called Beechwood Park. It was an old Manor, in fact they used the grounds to film *The Dirty Dozen* there. Anyway, my father used to deliver groceries up to the girls' school, and I learned to drive in their private driveway as well when I was a kid and below driving age. It was good to have a focus of a place, and around there I remembered that wonderful thing after it had rained and the sun comes out, the ground steaming and that smell. But basically it was just a story that I made up."

For Chris White, in particular, the summer of 1967 proved an incredibly creative period. Suddenly, he had taken a slight jump ahead of Rod Argent as The Zombies' main contributor of songs, ending up with seven tracks on the final *Odessey And Oracle* album against Argent's five. Furthermore, Rod Argent in one case found himself drawing on material written more than a year before, when "I Want Her She Wants Me" had been a single for The Mindbenders, helping them to stand on their own feet after their break-up with lead singer Wayne Fontana.

"Rod wrote this song," Chris White told me. "We just did a rough demo of it at the time. Rod hated The Mindbenders' version. They got all the chords wrong."

The dramatic climax during the recordings came in August when the band started work on a new Rod Argent song called "Time Of The Season". Rod Argent recalls having strong feelings about the song and its potential to become a hit, perhaps in the same league as "She's Not There". He was, of course, completely right. However, Colin Blunstone in particular didn't like this song at all and when it was time for him to add his lead vocal he simply refused.

"I was changing some phrasing in the singing," Rod Argent told me, "and he said to me, 'Look, if you're so bloody good, you do it.' I said, 'Come on, Colin. Come on, you do it.' I had to persuade him to do it."

Colin Blunstone: "I didn't think the song was attractive. I like it more now, but I certainly didn't at the time. I think Rod had written it quite shortly before we recorded it. I seem to remember learning the song on the morning before we recorded it. We recorded it in Studio 3 at Abbey Road. That was the studio we used most. The Beatles used Studio 2. I wasn't quite getting the melody right, and Rod was in the control room. He said, 'No, it's not quite right.' In the end it got quite heated. I said to him something on the lines of, 'If you're so bloody clever, you come in here and you bloody sing it.' And he said to me, 'You're the bloody singer. You stay at it until you get it right.' Those words might have been a bit worse, actually. Years later, of course, I'm very, very glad that I did stay there and sing it!"

I asked Chris White if he recalled Rod Argent being hurt by Blunstone's refusal to sing "Time Of The Season".

"No," he replied. "Rod, he was just surprised. We'd worked together for so long, we'd grown up together and you can have stupid arguments, but we never really fell out. It was just that it was a tiring session. We needed to get things done and we were in a hurry to get it over before the fellows in the white coats came in to do the studio."

Blunstone also told me how the group initially stumbled across the phrase which became the title of the song. As in so many other cases during The Zombies' career, it was coincidence and in fact a mistake that led them down the path to success:

"We were trying to transcribe the lyrics of 'Tracks Of My Tears', because we were going to do it on stage. Rod had written down, 'At the close of the season.' We said, 'What a great phrase.' Then we discovered it was really, 'If you look closer it's easy to see.' So we'd misheard it, but we thought we'd used it anyway and changed it into 'Time Of The Season'!"

Rod Argent: "I was sharing a flat with Chris at the time and I said to him, 'I've got the last track for the record.' I played it to him on a little grand piano I had in the room and I said, 'I think this could be a hit.'"

On 16 and 17 August "Care Of Cell 44", a Rod Argent song that would later open the new album, and White's "Brief Candles" were recorded.

"'Care Of Cell 44' was originally called 'Prison Song',"

Chris White remembered. "Then it was called 'Care Of Cell 69', and the American publishers said, 'Ooh no, you wouldn't be allowed to use that!'"

White's own "Brief Candles" featured vocal duties more democratically distributed than ever before.

"It came out of a book title," he told me. "I was searching around for inspiration and I though it would be lovely to have three different stories in this song. I suppose really it's just about the ridiculousness of trying to make reasons of things. Originally I wanted Colin to sing it on his own, and I put down the tune for his range. Then Rod said, 'Why don't we do one verse each?' I didn't think it was going to work when we were recording it but then, when we mixed it, I thought, 'Oh, yes!'"

Finally, the last song ever to be recorded by the original Zombies was laid down on 7 November 1967 and appropriately titled "Changes". This time there was a call for a vocal arrangement so elaborate that Paul Atkinson and Hugh Grundy were both invited to participate.

"We were all around two mikes," Colin Blunstone remembered, "and it was obviously coming towards the end of the session. The guys who moved pianos and things, they wore these long, white coats, it was very regimented – anyway, the red light was on and we were singing harmonies and these two guys came in and started wheeling this piano out of the studio right by. There we are singing our hearts out, and they were wheeling a piano out!"

Chris White: "That one was deliberately to do with chorus singing, chanting and not using drums. Instead, we were using congas – Hugh's playing. We were running out of tracks, so everybody sang on it, including Paul Atkinson. Rod wanted to put the low notes in, and Hugh and Paul sang that so that he and I could double-track a bit. We were very pleased with that."

The group now had finished recording all the tracks for their second album. It had been an exciting time, but also occasionally a rushed job.

Colin Blunstone: "The control room in Studio 3 at Abbey Road – you had to go out the side door and walk down a corridor to get into the actual studio, and I used to run because we were so tight on time. Also, at Abbey Road in those days sessions were 10 to 1, and they stopped at 1! And 2 to 5, and 7 until 10, and they definitely stopped at 10 because they got complaints from the neighbours about the noise. But I used to run, and it was really self-defeating because then, when I got to the mikes, I was out of breath and I had to wait to get my breath back. We were so up against it."

The pressures, however, weren't over yet. Most tracks had been mixed in mono during the recordings. However, 1967 represented a turning point in British recording methods and after the release of The Beatles' *Sgt Pepper*, which was seen as the first decently British stereo mix of a rock group (actually a debatable point since the mono version of that album is infinitely better), practices were radically changing. For The Zombies this meant that CBS suddenly expressed a demand for *Odessey And Oracle* to come out in both mixes – only they weren't willing to pay the extra expense.

"So we had to mix it in stereo," Chris White said, "and Rod and I paid for that out of our own pockets. That was extra difficult because we had no advances on that album, just the cost of the studio."

Since all the songs had been recorded on four-track equipment with just mono in mind, coming up with a stereo mix proved a difficult task and the result could not possibly be up to the quality of the mono version (though some tracks certainly work better than others). Nevertheless, when the group listened back to both mixes there was great satisfaction with the result:

"Rod and I were really knocked out with *Odessey And Oracle* afterwards," Chris White stated. "We were so pleased with all the sounds on it."

They had every right to be.

18

Odessey And Oracle – track by track

CARE OF CELL 44

Colin Blunstone: Lead vocals, backing vocals
Rod Argent: Harpsichord, Mellotron, backing vocals
Chris White: Bass guitar, backing vocals
Hugh Grundy: Drums

The song is built around four verses each consisting of four fairly long lyric lines (except verse 4 which is merely a shortened repetition of verse 3). There is a slightly unusual feature in that verse 2 follows straight after verse 1, with no vocal interlude or chorus in between. Furthermore, there is a bridge between verse 3 and verse 4.

The verses are built over a repetitive descending bass line, with the odd unusual chord thrown in, lifting and lowering moods in the well-established Zombies manner. There is in Argent's keyboard playing a tendency to sustain top notes for as long as possible, reminiscent of Matthew Fisher's organ work on "A White Shade Of Pale", the biggest hit in the charts at the time when most of *Odessey And Oracle* was recorded. Also worth noting is Chris White's elegant, melodic bass playing, reminiscent of Paul McCartney, and Hugh Grundy's precise, energetic drumming with some particularly exciting things going on in the bass drum department. Finally, Colin Blunstone's singing is wonderfully clean, open and intuitive as always.

The arrangement opens with a brief harpsichord solo introducing a chord sequence also used abundantly throughout the verses. It leads directly into verse 1, which has a dynamic build-up. Starting with just the harpsichord, drums and lead vocals, it adds in order, bass guitar, Mellotron strings [*see Glossary*] and, as the song enters verse 2, backing vocals (performing a simple harmony line above the bassline). There is then a break which finds the instrumentalists idle while a full vocal arrangement takes over, Beach Boys-style. This leads us into the chorus, which features the entire instrumentation augmented with big-sounding vocals.

Verse 3 continues where verse 2 left off, with the full band playing. Rod Argent performs a variation on the harpsichord, playing a rhythmic pattern reminiscent of Ravel's *Bolero*. The following break and chorus are the same as in verse 2.

Then the bridge comes in. Here the rôles of the instruments are reversed, as there is a sustained bass root, while Rod Argent plays series of descending chords on both harpsichord and Mellotron, some of these quite adventurous in the kind of Baroque-meets-jazz style made popular in the mid-sixties by artists such as Jacques Loussier and The Swingle Singers.

Verse 4, as already mentioned, is a shortened repetition of verse 3 followed by the now-familiar vocal break and chorus. This is succeeded by yet another break with variations which find the harpsichord taking over some of the previous duties from the vocalists. Finally there is a full-sounding finale formed by a series of descending chords and bass notes leading us back to the tonic chord, classical-style.

"Care Of Cell 44" is a highly original and individual song. It's not difficult to find in it inspirations from The Beatles (particularly the McCartney composition "For No One", which on the other hand appeared to be somewhat inspired by early Zombies), The Beach Boys, Procol Harum, then-contemporary jazz, and classical music. Nevertheless, out of all this comes something which is entirely whole, unique and fresh-sounding, even today.

Perhaps the most surprising feature is the lyric. As indicated in the title, it has the form of a letter written to someone who is in prison. Basically, the narrator expresses his joy now that his girlfriend will be released and – as you might have guessed – return "home" to him again.

For obvious reasons the combination of a seemingly positive love theme and a prison theme is pretty unlikely in a pop song (or anywhere else), and I can't recall this ever being used by any other songwriter. Previously, pop songs dealing with the subject of imprisonment had for the most part been rather bitter and twisted, if not downright aggressive – like Mose Allison's "Parchman Farm", Brown & Adderley's "Work Song", Bobby Fuller's "I Fought The Law" and Leiber & Stoller's "Riot In Cell Block No. Nine". In other cases they had been totally removed from reality into Pop-land, like Putman's "Green Green Grass Of Home" and Leiber & Stoller's "Jailhouse Rock".

What makes "Care Of Cell 44" even more remarkable is that since it is a male person singing we must assume that it is the female partner who is imprisoned. Years later, when Tony Orlando & Dawn's "Tie A Yellow Ribbon" turned yet another 1970s summer into a sonic depression, they made sure to keep the gender rôles within the traditional framework (as well as watering down the whole theme entirely).

Knowing that The Zombies arguably were the least bitter, twisted and aggressive group in the history of pop, it goes without saying that their prison song had to have a more positive outlook – the main theme being the excitement of seeing one's loved one again. Or is that entirely true? There are certainly indications in the lyric that by 1967 the world was changing, even here. First there is the knowledge we now have that the song at some point was to be titled "Care Of Cell 69", giving it sexual connotations which were immediately banned by the publishers. Second there are a few indications buried in the text that all is not really as well as it might look on the surface. I can't help feeling the author's repeated reassurances that from now on everything will be fine, that he has arranged things out here to her convenience and, particularly, his statement that there is a need for something to be sorted out, made up for, all carries a significant underlying tone of desperation. This is contrasted, and thus emphasised, by the almost cheerful arrangement and the whole performance (interesting also to notice that the expressed hope that everything will be "so nice" is planted right on top of the roughest, bluest mood-breaker of a chord in the entire song). All in all a very strange, intriguing composition indeed. Or, as Chris White put it to me:

"I haven't got a clue what that song is really about. It has always puzzled me."

As is indeed his right, I once again found Argent himself less than willing to explain his lyric much further than what is literally there on the paper, leaving it for the rest of us to exercise *our* right to read it whichever way is relevant to us (after all, we've all bought the song and paid for it). Personally, I have no doubt that any lyric dealing with prisons, mistakes that must be made up for, and a perhaps camouflaged worry over the future of some kind of relationship in reality must be based on pretty substantial emotions, first or second hand.

By all accounts, Rod Argent's own love life at this point was extraordinary sound and thriving. He had just met and fallen in love with dancer Cathy, with whom he is still married to this very day. However, we also know from Paul Atkinson that *his* relationship was going through a particularly difficult patch at the time. Is that why he isn't present on the recording? Is this song, in fact, in vague symbolic form about the crisis he was going through?

Whatever Rod Argent or any of his friends may have experienced or felt more than thirty years ago is arguably of little significance compared to the fact that his songs still have relevance today. Because of the very openness of the words, people can experience them in a manner that is considerably less confined to particular circumstances.

Finally, it is worth noting that structuring a song lyric in the form of a letter is a somewhat unusual idea; the most immediate comparison to me is The Jam's "Burning Sky" from their 1979 album *Setting Sons*. The connection between the two groups is not as farfetched as it may seem. Rod Argent told me about his surprise once when reading in a Paul Weller interview that Weller in fact counted *Odessey And Oracle* among his favourite albums:

"I loved The Jam. That hard, driving style. But I never thought they would have been inspired by us. It was very flattering, though."

Had Rod Argent over the years applied a slightly more analytical approach to his own work the parallels might have been less surprising to him. In an interview John Reed and Terry Rawlings conducted for *Record Collector* (No 154), Weller is quoted about a previously unreleased Jam song called "No One In The World":

"As to its structure, without getting too technical about this, there's a major-to-minor chord change which I used a lot around that time."

It is also interesting to notice that Weller around the same time often used to structure songs by starting them off with two verses instead of just one before introducing the chorus.

A ROSE FOR EMILY

Colin Blunstone: Lead vocals, backing vocals
Rod Argent: Piano, backing vocals
Chris White: Backing vocals

Simple beauty marks this melancholic song, arranged around just a grand piano and voices. The structure is: verse-chorus/verse-chorus/verse, with a few variations in each verse. The strong sense of economy becomes a prevailing mood throughout, capped by the fact that the third verse doesn't have a chorus. The piano is the only featured instrument, but even that is understatedly played in a sort of mock-beginner way, somehow supporting the lyrical theme of English village life, with old ladies living in a world of comfortable loneliness, rose gardens, missed opportunities. I can't help feeling that this is the sort of piano-playing you would expect to hear coming out of the open window of a thatched cottage near a village green on a summer Sunday around teatime. Rod Argent has admitted a certain inspiration from Paul McCartney's "Eleanor Rigby", yet as always he manages to turn his influences into something that is significantly his own.

Another function of the overall simplicity is to make room for a truly extraordinary vocal arrangement, with the backing vocals singing individual lines, weaving in and out of what quite simply is one of Colin Blunstone's most astonishing performances ever. As always with The Zombies, it is difficult to determine exactly how many voices there are. As already mentioned, there was something very fortuitous about the way particularly Argent and White's voices blended which made them sound like much more than just the two of them together. This, in fact, is yet another important key in understanding the group's artistic success.

MAYBE AFTER HE'S GONE

Colin Blunstone:	Lead vocals, backing vocals
Rod Argent:	Piano, backing vocals
Chris White:	Bass guitar, backing vocals
Hugh Grundy:	Drums
Paul Atkinson:	Acoustic and electric guitars

The first Chris White song on the LP, this is finally a full group performance built around a guitar riff. The piano is only faintly and occasionally heard, making room once again for a hugely impressive vocal arrangement. The structure is fairly traditional, with three verses interrupted by a bridge between the second and third verse. The minor-key chord structure and the descending bassline which dominate the verses promote a certain "Spanish" feel so often found in White's compositions, while the choruses feature the bass moving wildly around a fixed note with chords changing on top. In contrast, the bridge has an ascending bass line reminiscent of McCartney's "Here There And Everywhere".

Lyrically, this is melancholy and depression over a lost relationship taken to a new extreme where the writer conjures up images so dark that the original theme almost loses its importance and a more universal feeling of helplessness sets in. The sense of crushed naïvety and inability to forget is once again strongly amplified by Blunstone's pure, prepubescent delivery. This is yet another song so reminiscent of Nick Drake's output in the late sixties and early seventies that it makes you wonder to what degree Drake, whose vocal delivery is also highly reminiscent of Blunstone's, was influenced by The Zombies. (We shall probably never know, since Nick Drake was a recluse who gave very few interviews and died in 1974).

BEECHWOOD PARK

Colin Blunstone:	Lead vocals, backing vocals
Rod Argent:	Hammond organ, backing vocals
Chris White:	Bass, backing vocals
Hugh Grundy:	Drums
Paul Atkinson:	Electric guitar

For some time, this has been my own favourite track off the album. Everything is perfect here in true Zombies-style, from Atkinson's delicate tremolo guitar to Rod Argent's astonishing Baroque-inspired snippets of organ playing between the verses. The "rainy-day-in-June" feeling is emphasised by dense chord sequences moving up and down.

You could argue that this song could never have happened without Procol Harum; however, there are many things going on here which you won't find in any Harum song, particularly the rule-breaking chord structures and the overpowering vocal arrangement. Once again, the Beach Boys-influence is obvious, but it is worth noting that while The Beach Boys seem to have drawn their influences, with regard to vocal arranging, from typical American musical styles such as gospel and Doo-Wop, The Zombies build on a purely English tradition going all the way back to Elizabethan times. It's safe to say that the many years Rod Argent spent in St Albans School's choir were not wasted. As a result, where The Beach Boys' vocal arrangements seem to flow towards the listener and engulf him (an appropriate pun, I suppose), The Zombies' harmonies "ring out" as if in a cathedral, shifting between "ooh", "aah", even "la-la-la", interspersed by a complicated call and response technique which again is pure choral/Gospel tradition.

BRIEF CANDLES

Colin Blunstone:	Lead vocals, backing vocals
Rod Argent:	Lead vocals, backing vocals, piano, Mellotron
Chris White:	Lead vocals, backing vocals, bass
Hugh Grundy:	Drums
Paul Atkinson:	Electric guitar

Another overpoweringly beautiful Chris White composition, this time about learning to submit to your destiny and get through crisis situations enriched with a view of a larger perspective. It isn't quite clear whether it contains three different stories of certain similarity (theme: broken relationships), or the same story seen from three different angles. It doesn't matter, really. The first verse particularly contains the wise observation that it can be the person who breaks a relationship off who is the weaker part.

Musically, this is a typical *Odessey And Oracle* arrangement with its many starts and stops, quieter parts, energetic parts, vocal harmonies going in and out. Rod Argent continues to underplay – a genuine Ernest Hemingway of the grand piano! Grundy puts in vast amounts of enthusiasm and energy, while Paul Atkinson is his usual discreet self and contributes a few notes, eased in with the volume control during the choruses.

Perhaps the most striking feature here is a much more democratic distribution of vocal duties. It had always been one of Colin Blunstone's major complaints about how the group had been presented in the past that the two backing vocalists weren't brought more to the fore in the mixes, so with the band now in full control of the proceedings it is no surprise that there would be some kind of change in this area. As a consequence, both Argent and White are occasionally featured as lead vocalists, as in this song which starts off with Rod Argent singing the first verse and Blunstone not taking over until the chorus. Argent is a highly accomplished singer and also, as someone once put it to me, capable of "doing a pretty good Colin Blunstone". The second verse is sung by Chris White, who turns out to have a voice not unlike that of John Lennon. Finally, the third verse is sung by Blunstone throughout.

HUNG UP ON A DREAM

Colin Blunstone: Vocals, backing vocals
Rod Argent: Piano, Mellotron, backing vocals
Chris White: Bass, backing vocals
Hugh Grundy: Drums
Paul Atkinson: Electric guitar

Rounding off Side 1 we find The Zombies' "hippie anthem", which as already described, deals with quasi-religious experiences during meditation, instead of being drug-induced. The flowing feel of the music, brim-full of typical Rod Argent chord sequences persistently lifting and lowering the mood of the listener, supports the lyrical content. The guitar work represents Paul Atkinson's tasteful approach at its very best, including the rehearsed solo in the middle. No wonder he names this as his personal favourite track off the album.

Falsetto voices in the background more than ever before bring us right back to the Abbey of St Albans. This music quite simply is angelic, melting past and present into one. It has been said about The Beatles that the more they experimented with drugs, the more it seemed to bring them back to their childhood environment, as reflected in songs such as "Strawberry Fields Forever" and "Penny Lane". This song sees Rod Argent move in the same direction, albeit only in the musical framework, while lyrically, as so often before, there is a strong urge to solve some kind of personal struggle, a project which appears to have succeeded, at least momentarily. It is interesting that Rod Argent refuses to speak publicly against the use of so-called "mind-expanding substances", because in fact no statement could be stronger than this piece of music, written purely on a sensible, natural, hard-working method of achieving spiritual enlightenment.

On a more prosaic level, you could argue that the elaborate use of Mellotron makes this a period piece, but in fact it would take several years for the rest of the rock scene to catch up with what the group are on to here. A truly stunning achievement.

CHANGES

Colin Blunstone:	Lead vocals, backing vocals
Rod Argent:	Piano, Mellotron flutes, backing vocals
Chris White:	Backing vocals
Hugh Grundy:	Congas, backing vocals
Paul Atkinson:	Backing vocals

A quick look at the line-up on this Side 2-opener suggests a huge vocal arrangement. And indeed there is one, while the instrumental accompaniment is kept to an absolute minimum. One thing I found striking when analysing this album, after having known it by heart for years, was how few instruments and overdubs there actually are. It really has a big, overpowering sound but that is achieved by the use of only very basic resources, particularly multi-tracking human voices.

Another interesting feature on this one is the constant variations in the arrangement throughout the track. Up until now, even The Beatles' records had pretty much been a case of racing through three verses without many changes along the way apart from a small guitar solo or a bridge somewhere in between. Nothing wrong with that, but The Zombies obviously felt they had a few different ideas up their sleeve as to how pop songs could be constructed. Though this is a Chris White composition I would suggest that Rod Argent had a hand in shaping particularly the chords during Verse 2, which are jazzy variations on the chords already presented in the previous verse. Note also how the length of both choruses and verses are varied to add surprise and to ensure a perfect balance in the arrangement.

On the whole, subtlety and beauty characterise this song which once again establishes Chris White as one of the very best British songwriters of the sixties. Lyrically, it is a masterpiece as well, carefully hinting at the false values of material wealth. A setting which is somewhat fairy tale-inspired, yet also a poem that deals with the pain of seeing a friend change for the worse in front of your eyes. Do such juxtapositions make it psychedelic? I suppose they do.

The incorporation of Paul Atkinson and Hugh Grundy as backing vocalists once again points at a potential that was lost when the group split up soon afterwards.

I WANT HER SHE WANTS ME

Colin Blunstone:	Backing vocals
Rod Argent:	Lead vocals, harpsichord
Chris White:	Bass, backing vocals
Hugh Grundy:	Drums
Paul Atkinson:	Electric guitar

To my mind, three songs on *Odessey And Oracle* don't quite manage to stand up to the quality of the remaining album. These are "Maybe After He's Gone", "Time Of The Season" and this one.

Perhaps in this case it is because the song was written much earlier and somehow seems slightly dated, or perhaps it is Rod Argent's lead vocal that sounds a bit rough. Some time later, in the seventies, he would develop into one of my all time favourite lead singers, but in 1967 he still didn't quite pass muster, at least not to my mind. Lyrically, I also find that the "I'm-such-a-good-guy" theme is taken one step too far here.

The question is whether these three songs in any way diminish the overall sense of a high-quality, classic album? I don't think so. The flaws on this particular song lie mainly in parts of the performance and the lyric, as well as in the mix. However, as a piece of melody augmented with a set of chords it is of an exceedingly high standard, and towards the end of the track there are some very interesting things going on in the vocal harmony department. I'm sure that if the group had been granted more studio time they would have come up with an improved version.

THIS WILL BE OUR YEAR

Colin Blunstone:	Lead vocals
Rod Argent:	Piano
Chris White:	Bass
Hugh Grundy:	Drums
Paul Atkinson:	Guitar
	+ Horn ensemble

A strong, positive statement from Chris White in the lyrics here, supported by Colin Blunstone at his very best. Paul McCartney's "Penny Lane" could have been an inspiration – note the descending bassline and the horn arrangement, replacing vocal harmonies. However, this is pure White magic and pure pop, even to the extent where the second verse of the song is lifted a semi-tone to reinforce the excitement.

Where the early Chris White songs more often than not dealt with the agony of broken relationships, there is a tendency in some of his songs on this album (as indeed in Rod Argent's compositions) to write about these same feelings from a point where the crisis has been overcome and the future starts to look considerably brighter. There was throughout the "Swinging London" period in the mid-sixties an amazing feeling of positiveness and excitement which hadn't been particularly reflected in The Zombies' Decca production (perhaps yet another part of the explanation of why they didn't sell more records), but which now enters their idiom at full force.

A noteworthy feature here is Rod Argent's short but effective piano solo. Though he was by now becoming a highly accomplished keyboard soloist and occasionally would perform extended improvisations on stage, he still kept within the traditional pop song framework when recording (the one exception being "Time Of The Season"). That basically meant shaping your solos as a replication of the main melody line with a few variations thrown in and perhaps a slightly surprising ending.

BUTCHERS TALE (WESTERN FRONT 1914)

Rod Argent: Harmonium, oscillator
Chris White: Lead vocals
                + sound effects

When Chris White visited me to do the main interview for this book, we talked at some length about the First World War. There was obviously a common sympathy there, as the strong feelings he has about the issue compare well with how I myself feel about the Danish-German conflict in 1864 (White was surprised and interested to find that this in fact had also been a trench war, in some respects a historic forerunner for the 1914-18 confrontation). What pained us both was the way normal, everyday people had been brutally sacrificed on the altar of political stupidity and incompetence.

So far, I have based two full novels on the subject (in Danish, I hasten to add). However, I'm not sure that I have managed quite to capture the horrors as well as White does it here in "Butchers Tale". His supposed limitations as a lead singer, which he himself often points out, are undetectable. As with nearly all the songs on the album, everything is perfectly balanced, including the ultra-sparse arrangement, featuring Rod Argent's appropriately menacing handling of the mighty harmonium.

FRIENDS OF MINE

Colin Blunstone:	Lead vocals, backing vocals
Rod Argent:	Piano, backing vocals
Chris White:	Bass, backing vocals
Hugh Grundy:	Drums
Paul Atkinson:	Electric guitar

A short but tasty, Roger McGuinn-influenced guitar riff opens this track, which immediately takes us back into that strong feeling of "Swinging London". There is perhaps a certain melancholy in the narrator's sitting on the fence observing all the happy couples around him. Nevertheless, the overall spirit is positive.

White's experiences with meditation are reflected in the chant-like listing of names of friends. Otherwise, this is a pure pop song in the great Zombies tradition with descending basslines, unorthodox chord changes, precise and spirited drumming, tasteful keyboard and guitar playing, and superb performances from both lead vocalist and backing singers.

TIME OF THE SEASON

Colin Blunstone:	Lead vocals, backing vocals
Rod Argent:	Hammond organ, backing vocals
Chris White:	Bass, backing vocals
Hugh Grundy:	Drums
Paul Atkinson:	Guitar

Not my favourite track on the album, as already divulged. I suppose I somehow understand what Colin Blunstone had against this song at the time. Rhythmically it comes across as a somewhat downgraded "She's Not There", the chord structures and even the vocal arrangement occasionally have a peculiar, almost sinister feel to them, and the lyric seems to be about the narrator trying to get into some girl's panties by rapping about all the money he's got. Furthermore, the tempo and rhythmic accentuation are exceedingly difficult to solo over, and as a consequence Argent's Hammond work sounds slightly uncomfortable.

But, at least for me, these views are highly subjective and retrospective, because this is the one song on the album that more than anything signalled what lay ahead for Rod Argent with his own band later on, and it just occurs to me that the later ensemble did a somewhat better job playing in this particular style, incorporating more flowing structures and long, improvised keyboard solos (in fact, they used to do thundering "live" renditions of this very song).

However, listened to in the right context (and it doesn't take much tweaking of the mind), "Time Of The Season" is a fine song, and above all it has that "rounding-off" feel to it that any album would die for. Furthermore, it features a great performance from the band and – more surprisingly – their lead singer. It may have been that Colin Blunstone felt the group was going in completely the wrong direction here and that the recording came about in the middle of a row between him and Rod Argent, but his delivery is nevertheless entirely sympathetic to the song.

19

Vindication

A fter the recording of *Odessey And Oracle* there was a feeling within The Zombies that perhaps they were now able to make a new start. Listening back to the tapes, the two songwriters in particular felt very pleased with the work and during the final months of 1967 the group once again found themselves playing a string of small venues in their home country while waiting for the album to be released.

Things, however, were not well at all. Primarily, there continued to be a worrying lack of money going into the non-songwriting members' pockets.

"Colin and the others were really short of cash," Chris White told me. "So we said, 'Well, we'll see how this album goes.' They put a couple of singles out but we didn't really get anywhere in England. And America wasn't even going to put the LP out. So therefore we were quite disillusioned apart from maybe Hugh, who didn't mind – as long as he could play and look smart!"

Grundy himself recalls differently:

"I was under economic pressure too. You're still trying to earn a living, no matter that you're playing in a band and you're enjoying the music – it's still a living, and when the living creeps away, your commitments overtake you and it's a worry."

Gigging wasn't made any easier by Rod Argent's change from rather lightweight keyboards to a monstrous Hammond B3 with a big Lesley speaker cabinet [*see Glossary*]. Grundy again:

"Oh God, that bloody Hammond! It wasn't a split Hammond, it wasn't portable at all. It was a full-blown Hammond – 'Be careful about it, it's a beautiful piece of furniture. Careful as you come in the door!' But nevertheless, what a great sound. Always one of my favourite sounds, still is even now. I love to hear a Hammond played."

Colin Blunstone takes up the story:

"I can tell you it was hell trying to get it into places. Often it would be up little stairways and things, and they are so heavy. When it's a small staircase you can only get so many people around the instrument. It was very, very difficult."

During these last gigs, the group appear to have been performing some of the songs which had been recorded for the album, such as "Care Of Cell 44", "Friends Of Mine", "A Rose For Emily" and perhaps – this is debatable – "Time Of The Season".

"Rod and I have been thinking about this," Chris White said, "because when we played again in November 1997 [at the release of the *Zombie Heaven* box set] we didn't actually rehearse. The problem was that we couldn't remember how to end 'Time Of The Season'. And I pointed out to Rod, we actually never really played this on stage before. He played it with Argent in different versions and slowed it down, so he thought we had."

Two singles had so far been released in the UK during the autumn of '67, namely "Friends Of Mine"/"Beechwood Park" (in October) and "Care Of Cell 44"/"Maybe After He's Gone" (the following month; also released in the US), but both failed to make any impact. Things were getting tough and drab, and finally The Zombies played their last gig in mid-December, by all accounts at Keele University. It was then announced that they had split up.

There are almost as many accounts of the group's last few days as there are group members (with the largest degree of consistency being between Argent and White).

Rod Argent: "Colin basically, in his head, had left the band. He'd become very disillusioned with the fact that things weren't happening anywhere and I think he just got fed up with everything. Paul Atkinson felt the same too. Chris and I wouldn't break the band up, but we felt we couldn't carry on without Colin. I still think that's right. I had gradually become more confident as a lead singer, but even though I did bits and pieces of lead singing I always thought of Colin as the lead singer, which he was, and an indispensable part of the band. It comes to a point where, if people aren't really enthusiastic about it, there's no reason for carrying on."

Colin Blunstone: "I remember Paul saying he was going to leave. Then Rod said, 'If Paul wants to leave then I think the band should finish.' I didn't actually say anything, but Rod remembers me rather giving up, dragging my heels and not putting any energy into it, which is probably true. By the summer of '67 I thought in my heart it would just wind down on its own accord. By then the non-writers were fast running out of money. You have to take into account we were all living at home, we didn't have expensive cars or expensive holidays or anything. I literally hadn't got any money to live. So it seemed inevitable to me.

"Rod has said recently that I was losing interest, but really I was just drained. We'd played an awful lot and there'd been a lot of hard times and we hadn't had any hits to perk us up. The Philippines had been a fiasco. I still sometimes think that instead of that being the end of the band, it logically could very well have been the beginning of the band. We'd served our apprenticeship now, we'd had three years on the road, now we know the ropes. I do sometimes wonder what could have happened. But maybe there's the other side of it – maybe we'd had our time. Bands do have that, like The Beatles when they decided that it was the end. Maybe it wouldn't have been right to keep going.

"I think the killer for me was that there was no interest in the singles. So it just seemed a natural conclusion to disband."

Chris White: "I know that Rod did say, 'Well, if Colin and Paul want to leave we might as well knock it on the head.' You've got to really want to do it, and there was no sign at that time of bite in anything. We weren't earning the money. We weren't getting the gigs. The singles didn't sell. They weren't putting our records out in America any more. Nevertheless, Rod and I wanted to continue because we found that recording *Odessey And Oracle* was a great pleasure. But we agreed that if the others don't want to go on there's no point in finding new members. It wouldn't be the same thing any more. So it fizzled out that way."

Paul Atkinson: "I don't remember being the first one leaving. I remember it more as a group decision. When we rehearsed *Odessey And Oracle* and went in to record it, we discussed it as being our last record, that if this record didn't achieve some success we would break up. The singles came out from the record, in England, and failed. The album didn't come out until '68, but by the time it came out it was dead on arrival. We all knew that.

"I got married in October of '67. We were playing a few shows, and everyone was feeling very depressed. I think it's unfair to blame me for the break-up. I think we all agreed that if we didn't see some success from this record, we would disband. Maybe I said it out loud, because it was coming up to Christmas, it was the end of the year – where were we going? We weren't going anywhere. Maybe I was the first one to say it out loud, but we were all thinking the same. A very sad time."

Whatever the exact circumstances may be, by Christmas 1967 The Zombies has ceased to exist. Meaning, of course, that in some respects their life had only just begun.

* * *

The story of The Zombies' afterlife has been well covered elsewhere, particularly in Greg Russo's *Time Of The Season: The Zombies Collector's Guide*. It falls outside the framework for our story here (as do a number of songs released under The Zombies' name but in fact recorded by early incarnations of the group Argent).

Suffice to say that *Odessey And Oracle*, dressed in a subtle, but tasteful collage-sleeve by Chris White's friend Terry Quirk (who admits responsibility for the misspelling of "Odyssey"), came out to general indifference in Britain in April 1968 and was discovered more-or-less by accident by American Hammond wizard Al Kooper during a visit. Being signed to CBS himself Kooper started a long and hard battle for the album to be released in the US. This also resulted in a trio of singles taken from the album being put out in the States, none of them making any serious impact until the third one, "Time Of The Season", which during February 1969 stormed into the US charts where it stayed for thirteen months, topping at Number 1 in the *Cashbox* sales lists. Like "She's Not There", it is now regarded a landmark record and an-all time pop classic.

Pressures on the group to reunite on the back of this new, unexpected popularity were strongly rejected by Rod Argent, who by then had started putting together a new band, named after himself, with Chris White standing in the wings as fellow songwriter and producer. This group continued for almost ten years, after which Rod Argent has concentrated on a solo career. Today, he is back touring and recording with Colin Blunstone while also running his own studio, as is Chris White.

Paul Atkinson and Hugh Grundy both stopped working as professional players and took up other kinds of work within the recording industry. Atkinson today lives in Los Angeles and heads Capitol Records' re-issue department, while Grundy runs a pub.

Colin Blunstone, after a brief return to the insurance business in 1968, took up a solo career which still continues. Now in his fifties, he seems to be getting better and better.

During the three decades following The Zombies' demise Decca's archives have been repeatedly ploughed through by record company executives with the intention of unearthing old Zombies material and releasing it to a world of perpetually hungry fans. We have delved into these releases abundantly in this book, placing them in the chronological framework by date of recording, rather than of release.

The amount of interest that Decca showed in The Zombies' catalogue subsequent to "Time Of The Season" hitting the US charts, would probably have done the group a lot of good during the band's lifetime. However, there is also the argument that they were simply too understated, tasteful and sympathetic for their own good; that the world simply needed time to come fully to terms with The Zombies and realise their true status as one of the very best British acts from an era crammed with top quality rock groups.

May they never rest.

Glossary

Chords: A basic chord consists of three notes – a *root note*, a *third*, and a *fifth*. By lowering the third half a tone you shift from a major chord, which sounds "brighter", to a minor chord, which sounds "dark". While songs often include both major and minor chords, it is slightly unusual to let *the same* chord change between major and minor. An example is The Beatles' "In My Life", where the shift happens on the word "life", giving you the notion that the singer's life at some point has seen a change from a stage of contentment to a less cheerful condition.

Imagine taking the *fifth* in a chord and using that as *root note* for creating a new chord. Then do the same once again – take the *fifth* in this new chord and use that as yet another root note for yet another chord. You can repeat this only twelve times (since there are only twelve notes in the scale) – then you will find yourself back where you started; hence this process can be presented in the form of a cycle, known as *The Cycle of Fifths*.

Schematically speaking, when you are using chord-changes

that move you clockwise in the cycle of fifths you create a feeling of relief, of the mood being "dissolved", and even more so if you skip one or more links on the way. On the other hand, going anti-clockwise can create a feeling that "things are getting tougher" – for instance, a three-step-jump will be a bit like changing from a major chord into a minor.

A *diminished chord* is built by adding successive minor thirds to a root note. Such chords are nearly always used as links between two other chords. Since there are several options as to what can naturally follow after a diminished chord, they have a feeling of tension and uncertainty.

Major-seventh chords are basic chords with the addition of a fourth note, which is a semitone below the root note – this kind of chord makes for a slightly dreamy, naturalistic or melancholic feel associated with for instance impressionist composers; in Chris White's "Leave Me Be" it occurs appropriately at the point when the narrator reluctantly admits his inability to subdue his own feelings of loss.

Hammond organ: Unlike normal electric organs, Hammond's "tone wheel" models work according to a unique system where the sound is produced by cogwheels rotating in front of electromagnets, inducing an alternating current, which is sent through various electric filters and then amplified. With lots of mechanical parts moving inside it, an up-and-steaming Hammond shivers slightly and feels almost alive. More importantly (and unlike modern-day synthesizers, samplers and so forth) Hammonds also *sound* totally alive. Hammond's "tone wheel" organs went out of production some time in the early seventies, but even today they still feature heavily in the sound of many records and younger bands such as JTQ, The Charlatans, Corduroy and Kula Shaker.

Lesley speaker: To make a Hammond organ sound really good you need a Lesley speaker cabinet featuring internal motors and rotating loudspeakers.

Mellotron: Keyboard instrument invented in the mid-sixties and now seen as a forerunner for digital sampling technique. It uses real instruments and human voices pre-recorded on analogue tapes. On *Odessey And Oracle* Rod Argent uses the Mellotron in two different modes, Strings and Flutes.

Zombies original UK Discography

Singles
She's Not There/You Make Me Feel Good (Decca F11940, 1964)
Leave Me Be/Woman (F12004, 1964)
Tell Her No/What More Can I Do (F12072, 1965)
She's Coming Home/I Must Move (F12125, 1965)
Whenever You're Ready/I Love You (FF12225, 1965)
Is This The Dream/Don't Go Away (F12296, 1965)
Remember You/Just Out Of Reach (FF12322, 1966)
Indication/How We Were Before (FF12426, 1966)
Gotta Get A Hold Of Myself/The Way I Feel Inside (F12495, 1966)
Going Out Of My Head/She Does Everything For Me (F12584, 1967)
Friends Of Mine/Beechwood Park (CBS 2690, 1967)
Care Of Cell 44/Maybe After He's Gone (3087, 1967)
Time Of The Season/I'll Call You Mine (3380, 1968)
Imagine The Swan/Conversation Off Floral Street (4242, 1969)

EPs
The Zombies (Decca DFE 8598, 1965)

LPs
Begin Here (Decca LK4697)
Odessey & Oracle (CBS (S)63280)

CD box set
Zombie Heaven (Big Beat/Ace Records ZOMBOX 7)

The above covers all the music by The Zombies referred to in this
work. However, for considerably more elaborate discographical
detail see Greg Russo's *Time Of The Season: The Zombies
Collector's Guide*, available from Helter Skelter Books, London.

Index

About the Author

Claes Johansen was born in Copenhagen in 1957. He made his debut in the local literary scene at the tender age of seventeen with a short story printed in major publisher Gyldendal's monthly literary magazine. During the following decade he made his mark as a music critic, free-lance journalist, radio DJ and a member of Mod revival groups The Squad and Route 66, the latter recording an album in London in 1984 produced by Procol Harum's Matthew Fisher, who also contributed to the LP as a keyboardist and backing vocalist. The album was released in 1985, and the following year Gyldendal published Claes Johansen's first collection of short stories titled "Frygtelige Vera" ("Vera the Terrible"). A story from this collection was later translated into English and published in Canada, and other stories have subsequently been translated into both Swedish and Dutch.

Since 1986 Claes Johansen's literary career has produced on average more than one publication every year, primarily a series of much acclaimed novels. He is considered one of the most important current authors in a nation which traditionally produces world-class writers (Andersen, Blixen, Kierkegaard, Hoeg et.al).

In 1992 Johansen moved with his family to Devon in England, continuing his work in Danish while also taking up jobs as a sleeve-note writer for various British record companies such as Virgin/EMI, Angel Air, Retrowreck, and Voiceprint. In 2000 he published his first major work in English, a biography of legendary British rock act Procol Harum titled "Beyond The Pale", which received considerable praise in the established music press. The same year he started work on "Hung Up On A Dream", his second major publication in English. Currently he is working on a trilogy of novels taking place during the German occupation of Denmark between 1940-45.

Books in English:
Procol Harum - Beyond The Pale (SAF Publishing, London 2000)
The Zombies - Hung Up On A Dream (SAF Publishing, London 2001)

Record releases:
W/The Squad: Born In The Concrete/Polythene Chicks (7" single, Sonet, 1981)
W/Route 66: Back To The Garage (4-track cassette, 1982)
W/Route 66: Route 66 (LP, Telaeg 1985)
W/Route 66: Give Or Fake/Makin' Time (retrospective 7" single, Speak Louder Records 1994)
W/Route 66: Route 66 (CD issue of original LP w/bonus tracks, Angel Air 1997)

Books in Danish:
Frygtelige Vera og andre noveller (short stories 1986)
De sædvanlige tragedier (short stories 1987)
Ude og hjemme (a fairy tale 1988)
Alt hvad der er muligt (novel, 1988)

Smuk er døden, som I fik (novel, 1989)
Små slag (short stories, 1990)
Violinens historie (novel, 1991)
Uden for døren (essay, 1991)
Der er intet tilbage at benægte (short stories, 1994)
All the above published by Gyldendal, Copenhagen.
Tv!vleren (novel w/7" single, 1995)
I mørket bag min albue (essays, 1997)
Fodfolk (novel, 1997)
Som sne der faldt i fjor (novel, 1999)
The above four titles published by Aschehoug, Copenhagen.
Med munden (novel, Forum, Copenhagen 2000)

Titles available from SAF and Firefly Publishing

Necessity Is... The Early Years of Frank Zappa and the Mothers of Invention

by Billy James UK Price: £12.99

The early Mothers of Invention were a band of anarchic, free-spirited, musically telepathic mavericks headed by the unparalleled musical genius of Frank Zappa. Billy James recaptures those early years as remembered by Jimmy Carl Black, Roy Estrada, Bunk Gardner, Buzz Gardner and Don Preston. Completing the picture with anecdotes about other ex-members like Ray Collins, Lowell George, Art Tripp and Motorhead Sherwood, the book investigates the oddball humour that surrounded the Zappa entourage from 1964-1970.

Free At Last: The Story of Free and Bad Company

by Steven Rosen UK Price £14.99 (Due September 2001)

One of the greatest rock blues outfits of the early seventies, Free peaked with the seminal hit "All Right Now", centred around the gravel-laden voice of Paul Rodgers and the hauntingly resonant guitar playing of troubled soul Paul Kossoff. When Free disbanded, Rodgers and Free drummer Simon Kirke went on to form one of the seventies best-known supergroups - Bad Company.

Steve Rosen's history with both bands goes back a long way - he once drove Paul Rodgers to an Elvis Presley concert in his Triumph Herald, as well as covering Bad Company's formation in Rolling Stone. Using old and new interviews with members and associates, here at last is a portrait of two of rock music's treasures.

No More Mr Nice Guy: The Inside Story of the Alice Cooper Group

By Michael Bruce and Billy James UK Price £11.99

The dead babies, the drinking, executions and, of course, the rock 'n' roll.

Procol Harum: Beyond The Pale

by Claes Johansen UK Price £12.99

Claes Johansen has spent years researching Procol Harum's history from their early days through to international status as one of the biggest attractions of the 70s and 80s. "'Whiter Shade Of Pale' remained their milestone, and their millstone. But Procol were always a band of quality and in Beyond The Pale they finally have the book they deserve." Mojo.

An American Band: The Story of Grand Funk Railroad

By Billy James UK Price £12.99

One of the biggest grossing US rock 'n' roll acts of the 70s - selling millions of records and playing sold out arenas the world over. Hype, Politics & rock 'n' roll - unbeatable!

Wish The World Away: Mark Eitzel and American Music Club

by Sean Body UK Price £12.99

Sean Body has written a fascinating biography of Eitzel which portrays an artist tortured by demons, yet redeemed by the aching beauty of his songs.

Go Ahead John! The Music of John McLaughlin

by Paul Stump UK Price £12.99

One of the greatest jazz musicians of all time. Includes his work with Miles Davis, Mahavishnu Orchestra, Shakti. Full of insights into all stages of his career.

Lunar Notes: Zoot Horn Rollo's Captain Beefheart Experience

by Bill Harkleroad and Billy James UK Price £11.95

For the first time we get the insider's story of what it was like to record and play with an eccentric genius such as Beefheart, by Bill Harkleroad - Zoot himself!

Meet The Residents: America's Most Eccentric Band

by Ian Shirley UK Price £11.95

An outsider's view of The Residents' operations, exposing a world where nothing is as it seems. It is a fascinating tale of musical anarchy and cartoon wackiness. Reprinted to coincide with the recent world tour.

Digital Gothic: A Critical Discography of Tangerine Dream

by Paul Stump UK Price £9.95

For the very first time German electronic pioneers, Tangerine Dream mammoth output is placed within an ordered perspective.

The One and Only - Homme Fatale: Peter Perrett & The Only Ones

by Nina Antonia UK Price £11.95

An extraordinary journey through crime, punishment and the decadent times of British punk band leader, Peter Perrett of The Only Ones

Plunderphonics, 'Pataphysics and Pop Mechanics

The Leading Exponents of Musique Actuelle

By Andrew Jones UK Price £12.95

Chris Cutler, Fred Frith, Henry Threadgill, John Oswald, John Zorn, etc.

Kraftwerk: Man, Machine and Music

By Pascal Bussy UK Price £12.95

New edition for 2001 - completely updated and revised. The story behind one of the most influential bands in the history of rock.

Wrong Movements: A Robert Wyatt History

by Mike King UK Price £14.95

A journey through Wyatt's 30 year career with Soft Machine, Matching Mole & solo artist.

Wire: Everybody Loves A History

by Kevin Eden UK Price £9.95

One of British punk's most endearing and enduring bands combining Art and Attitude.

Tape Delay: Confessions from the 80s Underground
by Charles Neal UK Price £15.00
Marc Almond, Cabaret Voltaire, Nick Cave, Chris & Cosey, Coil, Foetus, Neubauten, Non, The Fall, New Order, Psychic TV, Rollins, Sonic Youth, Swans, Test Dept and many more...

Dark Entries: Bauhaus and Beyond
by Ian Shirley UK Price £11.95
The gothic rise of Bauhaus, Love & Rockets, Tones on Tail, Murphy, J, and Ash solo.

Gentle Giant – Acquiring The Taste
by Paul Stump. UK Price: £16.99 (limited edition hardback)
Based around the Shulman brothers, Gentle Giant quickly acquired a large cult following the world over. Their music has endured over time and new generations are as entranced by their intricate sound as were audiences of 30 years ago.

Poison Heart: Surviving The Ramones
by Dee Dee Ramone and Veronica KofmanUK Price £11.95
Dee Dee's crushingly honest account of life as junkie and Ramone. A great rock story!

Minstrels In The Gallery: A History Of Jethro Tull
by David Rees UK Price £12.99
At Last! To coincide with their 30th anniversary, a full history of one of the most popular and inventive British bands.

DANCEMUSICSEXROMANCE: Prince - The First Decade
by Per Nilsen UK Price £12.99
A portrait of Prince's reign as the most exciting black performer to emerge since James Brown and Jimi Hendrix.

Soul Sacrifice: The Santana Story
by Simon Leng UK Price £12.99
In depth study of seventies Latin guitar legend whose career began at Woodstock through to a 1999 number one US album.

Opening The Musical Box: A Genesis Chronicle

by Alan Hewitt UK Price £12.99

Drawing on hours of new interviews and packed with insights, anecdotes and trivia, here is the ultimat compendium to one of the most successful and inventive bands of the modern rock era.

Blowin' Free: Thirty Years Of Wishbone Ash

by Gary Carter and Mark Chatterton UK Price £12.99

Packed with memorabilia, rare photos, a definitive discography and utilising unprecedented access to band members and associates, Gary Carter and Mark Chatterton have charted the long and turbulent career of one of England's premier rock outfits.

To Hell and Back with Catatonia

by Brian Wright UK price £12.99

Fronted by the brassy, irrepressible Cerys Matthews, Catatonia exploded onto the British pop scene in 1998. Author Brian Wright has been an ardent Catatonia supporter since their earliest days. Drawing on first hand experience, new interviews and years of research, he charts their struggle from obscure 1993 Cardiff pub gigs to the Top Ten.

The Manic Steet Preachers – Prole Art Threat

by Ben Roberts UK price £12.99 (Due Spring 2002)

Prole Art Threat takes a fresh look at one of the most controversial and important bands of the recent rock era. Using new research and interviews with band insiders, 21-year-old Ben Roberts charts the Manics' progress from Blackwood misfits to rock iconoclasts.

U2: The Complete Encyclopedia

by Mark Chatterton UK Price £14.99 (Due Nov 2001)

Here at last is the book that all completists, fans and U2 reference hounds have been waiting for. Hot on the heels of the huge success of Firefly's ultimate guide to all things Genesis, we can now announce the publication of the complete A to Z of the career of U2. Fully up-to-date, it documents the band's historical details from their early days in Dublin, to the current world tour.

Mail Order

All SAF and Firefly titles are available by mail order from the
world famous Helter Skelter bookshop.
You can either phone or fax your order to Helter Skelter on the
following numbers:

Telephone: +44 (0)20 7836 1151 or Fax: +44 (0)20 7240 9880
Office hours: Mon-Fri 10:00am - 7:00pm,
Sat: 10:00am - 6:00pm, Sun: closed.

Postage prices per book worldwide are as follows:

UK & Channel Islands	£1.50
Europe & Eire (air)	£2.95
USA, Canada (air)	£7.50
Australasia, Far East (air)	£9.00
Overseas (surface)	£2.50

You can also write enclosing a cheque, International Money Order,
or registered cash. Please include postage. DO NOT send cash.
DO NOT send foreign currency, or cheques drawn on an overseas
bank. Send to:

**Helter Skelter Bookshop,
4 Denmark Street, London, WC2H 8LL, United Kingdom.**
If you are in London come and visit us, and browse the titles
in person!!

**Email: helter@skelter.demon.co.uk
Website: http://www.skelter.demon.co.uk**

For the latest on SAF and Firefly titles check the SAF website:
www.safpublishing.com

saf publishing

www.safpublishing.com